it's not you,

THE ZERO TOLERANCE APPROACH TO DATING

it's him

Dr. Georgia Witkin

Broadway Books

New York

PRINTED IN THE UNITED STATES OF AMERICA

Visit our Web site at www.broadwaybooks.com

Library of Congress Cataloging-in-Publication Data
Witkin, Georgia.
It's not you, it's him : the zero tolerance approach to dating / Georgia Witkin.
p. cm.
1. Mate selection. 2. Dating (Social customs) 3. Man-woman relationships. 4. Women—Psychology. I. Title.

HQ801.W77 2006
646.7'7'082—dc22

2005051229

ISBN 0-7679-2050-3

10 9 8 7 6 5 4 3 2 1

To my beloved mother,

Dr. Mildred Hope Witkin

contents

acknowledgments

To Mel Berger, for thinking of me for this project and supporting it every step of the way.

To Howard Kaminsky, for trusting me with his concept and cheering it on.

To Kris Puopolo, my editor and collaborator, for her midnight notes and constant creativity.

To Beth Haymaker, for all her extra effort.

To Joanne Benjamin, Connie Freeman, Bobbie Gallagher, Roberta Greenberg, Carol Hankin, E. D. Hill, Helene Kaplan, Arlene Lazare, Gwen Marder, Edith O'Donnell, Mary Turko, and Lauren Day, for their fabulous female friendship.

To Sheldon, Mikey, and Justin, for their kindness and generosity.

To Kimberly, for always caring, sharing, and for bringing Travis, Jake, and Ty into my life.

And to Mike, for love, laughter, and our life together.

Thank you.

preface

Why is this book for single women? Because we think about relationships, and talk about relationships, much more than single men do. And when things go wrong, we're also much more likely to blame ourselves! We ask ourselves "What's wrong with me?" "What did I do?" "What didn't I do?" What should I have done differently?" and "What should I do differently next time?"

Well maybe, just maybe, you are not the problem. Maybe, just maybe you'd still be single *even if you were perfect*. Maybe the men you're meeting have the problems. Maybe it's not you, it's him! Maybe if you stop blaming yourself, your approach to dating will become more practical and sensible and successful.

Actually, there's no "maybe" about it. Your aunt in Florida, your married brother, and your gym friends are wrong—you are not single because you're too picky, too pushy, or a princess. Besides, even if you were, picky, pushy princesses get married every day. And so will you. So let's get real and get you the life you want.

This book will teach you to

Assume that you're perfect as you are . . . perfectly lovable, that is!

Assume that you're entitled, therefore, to be loved by a perfect man . . . just as you always wanted.

Assume, however, that there is no perfect man . . . in the whole world, and every man you meet will be imperfect . . . in many ways.

Assume that if he doesn't find you lovable, that's proof that he's imperfect . . . at least for you.

In other words, always assume that it's not you . . . it's him!

But what about those guys who *do* find you perfectly lovable as you are? Suppose you aren't sure if he is what you want. Suppose you're wondering if there's a better match out there. Want to know if you should stay or go? When to give it a test or give it a rest? It's not as difficult as we've all been making it!

There are real signs and signals that lead the way.

There are real tests that give us the information we need.

There are real rules for sorting it out.

Now, want to know when it's time for zero tolerance? Want to know when it's time to take more time? Want to know when to have fun and when to run? *Read on!*

1 Assume You're Perfect

You're single, and your mother says you're too hard to please, your sister says you're too assertive, and your friends say you should play hard to get. You argue with them, but you suspect that they may be right. You've begun to believe that you're too picky, too pushy, or a princess. Right? Well, here's a news flash: even if they are right, it doesn't matter. The odds are that you would still be single even if you were perfect!

The real problem isn't you at all. It isn't your hair, your weight, your job, your hobbies, your accent, your family, or your perfume. It isn't that you're too choosy, cautious, or combative. It isn't that you're too shy or too social, too spoiled or too stingy, too career-minded or too marriage-minded. Somewhere, there is a guy for you . . . actually, many guys. But all you need is one. And he'll fall in love with you as you are. To him you'll be perfectly lovable. Take the case of Marianne:

> Marianne just got engaged. Her friend told me that Marianne ran into an old flame (her Mr. Big!) at a party and they started seeing each other again, for what must be the fourth time. Her friend said she was in despair that Marianne would do this to herself again. But listen to this!
>
> They went on vacation together to a pricey resort, and this time Marianne decided to stop trying so hard to please him, and instead she decided to do whatever she wanted to do (sleep late, go to the spa). If he went to play golf at dawn, well, so be it. She was prepared to be dumped again and was just going along for the ride. But instead of breaking her heart again, he proposed!

Had Marianne's boyfriend proposed this time because he thought she was too needy before and now saw her as more independent? Had things changed because she was trying too hard before and now was more relaxed? Had her boyfriend found her too available before and now hard to get? Her friends had plenty of theories about the relationship. But it was none of these things. Marianne asked him. She said, "Why now?" "Well," he said, "I'm over forty now, and I'm ready to settle down." He said he'd always loved her but just wasn't ready. It wasn't her—it was him!

This floored Marianne's friend. Why? Because she realized that she was doing exactly what most single women do to themselves—she blamed Marianne for her boyfriend's reluctance to move ahead, when it really had very little to do with her. She was perfectly lovable all along; she was just dating someone who wasn't perfectly ready.

The Primary Principle

The truth is, there's someone for everyone, and eventually every one of us will find our prince. *And we don't need to change who we are to make that dream come true*. We do, however, need to change how we date, how we see men, and, most of all, how we see ourselves. We need to understand just when the problem is not us. We need to understand just how the problem is not us. And we need to understand just why the problem is not us. But it's not easy to stop blaming yourself. After years of having the wrong ideas about dating and going about it the wrong way, it takes practice to get it right, but you can do it. What follows are the strict directions, exercises, tests, and drills that will help you find a fairy-tale ending while dating in the real world. They are the same psychological prescriptions I've given to patients for almost two decades . . . and they really work!

Dating the wrong way is trying to reinvent yourself again and again, and then changing yourself still more. All that time and effort focused on yourself, blaming yourself, being dissatisfied with yourself, is a huge drain. Instead, it's time to get practical and realistic.

Dating is hugely simplified when you assume that you're perfect but that no man is ever going to be. When you assume that you're perfect, you realize that 90 percent of your dating efforts—constantly reinventing yourself to seem like Ms. Right for Mr. Wrong—have been a waste. The problem was never you. It was him.

Write this principle on a Post-it and stick it to your mirror and refrigerator, write it on a card and put it in your desk, print it in your daily planner, and make it a screen saver.

It's not you, it's him.

It should become your mantra and your credo. Repeat it to yourself at least five times a day. Why? Because what we think leads to what we feel and do. Does that surprise you?

Choose What You Think

Most of us grew up believing our emotions rule us. We were taught that when we're feeling "down," we have "down" thoughts and behave that way. When we're feeling "up," we have "up" thoughts and act "up." But psychology's biggest discovery of the past two decades is that it really works the other way around. We can choose what we think, and what we choose to think leads to how we feel and what we do! I'll say it again. *You can change what you feel and do by changing what you think.*

This is great news. This means you can change the way you *feel* about dating the minute you change the way you *think* about dating. This means you can change the way you feel about yourself the minute you change the way you think about yourself. It doesn't take years of therapy, counseling, or analysis. You don't have to review all your "issues," work out your family relationships, or sort through your "baggage" first. *Things can change today.*

When you think differently, you will feel different. When you feel different, you will act differently. Sounds too simple. Just try it. Researchers at Harvard's Thorndike Lab find that it works. Cognitive and behavioral therapists find that it works. Alcohol and drug rehab counselors find that it works. Physical therapists find that it works. Ministers, priests, rabbis, and spiritual advisors find that it works. My patients, clients, and I find that it works.

Turn Dating on Its Head

Now take this new approach and apply it to dating. As I said before,

Assume that you're perfect as you are . . . perfectly lovable, that is.

Assume that you're entitled, therefore, to be loved by a perfect man . . . just as you always wanted.

Assume, however, that there is no perfect man . . . in the whole world, and every man you meet will be imperfect . . . in many ways.

Assume that if he doesn't find you lovable, that's proof that he's imperfect . . . at least for you.

In other words, always assume that it's not you . . . it's him!

Once you start assuming that you are perfectly lovable just the way you are, everything will change—how you think will change how you feel, which will change what you do.

You'll start to look at each new man through your eyes instead of looking at yourself through his. You'll see dating as your opportunity to see if he's someone who might become special to you or someone you should say *sayonara* to.

Along the way, you may be tempted to fall back on your old doubts about yourself, especially if you've had some problems with romance lately. But you can practice your new thinking by focusing clearly on the primary principle:

It's not you, it's him.

Once you make that assumption, everything men say and do will be information about *them*, not you! If a guy doesn't treat you as perfectly lovable, you'll feel like a curious observer, a stern judge, or an amused bystander instead of wondering what you did wrong. You'll wonder what's wrong with him, not what's wrong with you.

Once you make that assumption, if a guy does treat you as perfectly lovable, you'll respond with grace and not jump in before he changes his mind or act as if he's your only chance at marriage.

Once you make that assumption, you'll stop blaming yourself for being single! It's never been about you. It's always been about him. If he didn't follow up, it's his problem.

If he didn't appreciate you, it's his problem.

If he didn't commit to you, it's his problem.

You'll stop asking yourself why. It may have been timing, a previous entanglement, or his insecurity. You may never know. What you will know is that it's a numbers game, and it's time for you to move on. If he didn't like your humor, you'll look for someone who does. If he didn't like your friends, you'll find someone who does. If he didn't like your family, you'll be sure the next guy does. You'll stop trying to change yourself when romance fails, and you'll change partners instead. You'll choose to fall in love with someone who's madly in love with you.

You'll react with zero tolerance when you receive zero.

It might be the opposite of anything you've ever done since you started dating. But that's the point. And the time to start is now!

2

Do What You Want, Wear What You Want, Go Where You Want

Maybe you've heard from your mother, friends, or dating manuals that the key to finding a guy is to "go where the boys are." Hang out at a sports bar, sign up for a wine-tasting class, or take up boating. All that's fine if you like rooting for the home team, sipping wine, or sailing the open seas. But if you don't, forget about it. Somewhere there is a guy for you, and you don't have to find him at the gym if you hate working out. By doing things you think guys like but that you don't, you're assuming you're not perfectly lovable with the interests that you already have. You'll soon find out that it's not your interests that are preventing you from meeting men.

Faking It Doesn't Work

What happens if you sign up for wine tasting just to find a guy, even though you can't tell red from white without looking, and you're fine with that? Or you tell a guy you meet that you like the same hobby he does just to make a connection? Well, you're not showing him the true and perfectly lovable you. Instead, you're pretending. Worse than that? You're assuming that you aren't good enough for him as is. (You don't see many men joining a book clubs or taking spinning classes just to meet a woman.)

Now, say you start dating that guy. Either you'll have to keep up the "I love wine" act forever, which would be tough, or you'd have to confess. Telling him the truth at such a late date would send the wrong message again: that you don't believe that who you are is just fine. The right message? "I can be me."

To make matters worse, after a while you're likely to realize that you don't *really* connect, since the common ground you started on was all pretend.

Here's what happened to Audrey when she faked it:

> Audrey started dating Joe. He loved fishing and anything to do with the water. She got seasick just watching *The Love Boat* (well, almost). But to keep the flames burning she pretended that she loved

> the water and the activities that went with it. After a few months, Joe booked their first vacation together: a trip to a remote island off the Bahamas. Not only was she horribly seasick on their daily fishing trips, but she was also bored. There was nothing else to do on the island but water sports. It was no vacation, and Audrey spent her precious time off from work throwing up in the ocean.

Think of what your (happily) married friends told you when they met The One: "It's like we speak the same language." "I'm so comfortable with him." "He really gets me." "He likes me just the way I am." That's what your goal is, and the only way to find the guy who loves you just the way you are is to be . . . just the way you are.

If a guy's really into you and finds you perfectly lovable, you don't have to be a carbon copy of him. He can be him. You can be you. And he can still be madly in love with you even though he goes fishing and you go shopping.

Do his thing if you care about him and want to do him a favor—it will make both of you feel good.

Do his thing if you care about him and he asks you to do him a favor—it will get you some IOU points and show him that you're a sport.

Do his thing if the two of you are compromising: he'll go bike riding with you, so you'll go fishing with him—it will tell you if he *can* compromise and if he appreciates your flexibility.

Do his thing if you think you may actually like a new activity or change your mind about an old one—and let him know you're testing it out, so that he will try hard to make it great and he won't expect you to do it forever (unless you find you love it).

Do his thing if you find him so perfectly lovable that you want to and he finds you so perfectly lovable that you know *you don't have to.*

Rx: Do his thing if it's a favor or fun—never if it's a fake.

Little Pleasures

How long has it been since you were first ready to meet "him"? Two years? Five years? Ten years? There's another reason to do what you want, besides becoming more perfectly you. You may find out once you meet him that the time you spent single may have been your only chance to do exactly what you want!

> Carla was lying in bed next to Matt and listening to all the noises he made while he slept. His thumb was still on the TV remote channel button, and if she tried to take it or turn the TV off, he'd wake up and say he wasn't finished watching. Tomorrow she had to wait for the carpet cleaning service, edit an article for the magazine she worked for, then cook and freeze Swedish meatballs for her sister-in-law's

> birthday party next weekend. Great. She remembered life before Matt. She remembered eating Oreo cookies in bed while she watched *Sex and the City* reruns, sleeping spread out on the bed, shopping for sale shoes during lunch, and seeing two movies on a Saturday. Why had she always felt that her life hadn't begun yet? Her life then seemed like a vacation to her now! Not that she'd trade Matt in for those Saturdays. But she'd sure like one again every once in a while.

Think of Carla and don't think of one minute of your single life as wasted time or second best. Instead of focusing on what you *don't* have at the moment, a mate, focus on what you *do* have at the moment, freedom to do exactly as you please. Remember, what you feel is the result of what you think, and you can choose what you think. So choose to think of your single life as an opportunity for little pleasures, and enjoy every minute. This is not waiting time, it's your time. Perfectly lovable women can have perfectly great times all the time.

Trust Your Interests

Sign up for that tennis clinic or film appreciation class you've wanted to take, or hit the museums on weekends if that's what you love—and, yes, you might meet a guy. If you do, you'll start out knowing that you have at least one real interest in common. But if you don't meet someone, who cares? Single life is all about finding out what you enjoy and about making yourself more truly *you*. The most efficient way to find someone who loves you exactly the way you are is to *be* exactly who you are.

> Judy was an active woman who wanted to meet someone who was also into health and fitness. She signed up for a running club to train for the New York Marathon. Yes, she joined because she wanted to meet a guy. But that wasn't the only reason. She loved being fit and healthy, and she loved to run and had always wanted to do a marathon. After pounding the pavement for several weeks, she did fall in love—with a guy who shared her goal: to log twenty-six miles. And that wasn't their only connection—they both cared about staying fit, were vegetarians, and did other sports.

Have you noticed how often other similar interests or qualities go along with the initial one? Another great reason for doing what you want.

But even if Judy *hadn't* met her running mate, she'd still have gotten something out of lacing up her sneakers. She got to indulge in one of her passions and complete a long-time goal. It would have been worth it either way.

Look at it this way: when we go on dates, we act like dates and find dates; when we go to singles bars, we act like singles and find singles; but when we go our own way, we find others who are going the same way. In other words, when we go on with our life, we find life partners. So be out there, going where you love to go, wearing what you love to wear, doing all you love to do, and men will find you. Then you can choose your great mate from among them.

3 Don't Ask Why

Remember Marianne? She spent years asking herself why, why, why the men she loved didn't love her back. What was wrong with her? Was it the three P's? Was she too picky, too pushy, or a princess? In Marianne's case, she *is* a princess, but she still found someone to love her. That's my point. Finding the reason doesn't matter, because it's not about you. Sure, you may have some teeny weeny imperfections, but that's not why you're still single. You're perfectly lovable to many men as you are. (We sure take imperfect men as they are!) If the guy you met last night isn't one of these many men, he's the one with the problem. I'll say it again. It's not you, it's him.

Why do we feel the need to ask why? Women in particular are always looking for explanations in their lives as well as relationships. We see it as our job to fix people, things, and potential problems, so naturally we do it when we date, too. If it hasn't worked out, it doesn't seem like it's going to work out, or we're afraid it won't work out, we try to get control of the situation by thinking there is something wrong with us. It gives us some sense of power. Since we can't really change the guy, we start working on ourselves. (A clear violation of the assumption that you're perfectly lovable . . . just as you are.)

But if the relationship is truly over, or never got started, it does no good to waste time asking why and wondering what's wrong with you. Zero tolerance for guys who give you zero is critical, but zero tolerance for self-blame is even more crucial. Self-blame can make us physical and emotional wrecks. It distracts us from moving on and from looking for a guy who *does* find us perfectly lovable so that the next time around it's not so much work.

> Jenny learned the hard way, as many of us do. When she was in high school, her first serious boyfriend suddenly dumped her. She was stunned. She kept thinking and thinking about it. She had trouble sleeping and concentrating in school and at her part-time job. Finally, after asking her mother for the twentieth time what she should do, her exasperated mom said, "You can't *make* the boy love

you. Find someone else. There will always be another one."

Jenny's mother's shock therapy worked. Her words may seem tough, but there's a reason that they say you should listen to your mother. She was right! You can't make someone love you—and you shouldn't try. You may never know. Never understand. Jenny didn't like the idea, but she accepted that she needed a new boyfriend. And she found one, and then another. She is now married but tells her single friends, "There'll always be another one—move on. Don't waste your time asking why."

Ask What

Don't ask why. Ask *what*. What do you want from a man who loves you? And what did you get instead? That is all you need to know. Think about it. When you were dreaming about Mr. Right, did he forget to call you for weeks on end? Did he see other women? Did he spend more time with his buddies drinking beer and shooting pool than with you? Of course not. So he can't be all that "right" for you, can he? Your dream man would never treat you so badly. So it follows that you should never let a real-life man treat you so badly either.

It's time to see him as he is—*Mr. Wrong*—not as you want him to be. Remember to look at his behavior as information about *him*, not as information about *you*. What did the behavior reveal about his attitudes, considerations, or intelligence? Was he as "ideal" as you had imagined? If you had not been the woman involved, what would you have thought of his behavior?

> A few weeks after Jordana had enough of Randy and broke up, she started having second thoughts. That's when her best friends decided it was time for a romance reality check. They staged an intervention over margaritas at their favorite Mexican restaurant and asked Jordana why in the world she was reconsidering her breakup with Randy. "But it wasn't so bad. He's hot. He could be very sweet. Maybe I should have given him more time," she said. "Forget it," they said. "Tell us what you didn't like about him," they insisted. At first she couldn't do it, so they reminded her of the times he didn't call her, the time he took off with his friends for Vegas without even telling her he was leaving town for the weekend, and the time she suspected him of cheating. "Ask yourself if this is what you wanted from that relationship," said her closest friend. Well, of course it wasn't. No one goes into a relationship expecting to be hurt. "It's not you, it's him," they told her. "You did everything right. He's the one who didn't treat you or your relationship with respect." Faced with the cold hard facts, Jordana stopped glamorizing their time together. When she thought about the ways things really were instead, she knew she was better off without him. "Next time," her friends told her, "ask your-

self what you want from him." She did. It was reliability and predictability, and next time she got it.

Decide what *you* want before your next relationship. I'm not suggesting a list—you're dating people, not adjectives. I am suggesting a lot of self-knowledge, the more the better. If you really want a fun time with no strings, fine, go for it. But if you're looking for a serious contender for Mr. Right, you have to know what's right for you. Remind yourself:

You are perfectly lovable (even if you don't feel that way at the moment).

You are, therefore, entitled to a loving (and perfectly lovable) man . . . as you always wanted.

And, finally, the primary principle:

It's not you, it's him.

Why Do We Ask Why?

We ask why because it's natural. Women seem to have a great capacity for empathy—the ability to put themselves inside other people's heads. We usually use it for good. When someone we love is upset, we ask ourselves "What does she feel?" "What can I do?" or "What would I want someone else to do if I was feeling bad?" But sometimes we use this capacity against ourselves. We put ourselves inside others' heads and try to look at ourselves through their eyes.

It's called spectatoring, and even though we can never really know how we look to others, we constantly try. And we usually do it very critically. Soon our view of our world is "outside in," looking at ourselves through everyone else's eyes, rather than "inside out," looking out at the world through our own eyes.

Actually, research finds this difference between males and females starts very young. By about eleven years of age, boys automatically take credit for things that go right, whereas girls think they just got "lucky." On the other hand, when something goes wrong, boys label it as "inconvenient," whereas girls take responsibility by saying, "What did I do?"

By the time we're twenty-one, we're masters at this. If a guy likes us, we feel we're lucky instead of entitled to his feelings because we're perfectly lovable. Most men, on the other hand, seem to walk around feeling perfectly lovable all the time. If a relationship doesn't work out, it's not *their* fault. Something was wrong with the woman, not them. (That may be why so many men describe their ex-girlfriends as "psycho." They think the girls must be crazy not to love them!) We women need more of that thinking. Here's one way perfect women can learn from imperfect men!

Does all this mean that we should never work on ourselves at all? Of course not. But here's the rule: make changes only to make yourself happy—not to get the guy or so that the next guy will find you more lovable. And at the very least, every time you don't become some man's loved one, make sure you treat yourself as your *own* loved one.

Take good care of yourself until your perspective and energy are restored. Treat yourself just as you would have liked him to treat you. Reassure yourself that you are worth it. And don't ask why. The only explanation you need is ***it's not you, it's him.***

4 Don't Apologize

For most of us, it's our worst trait. We walk around constantly saying, "I'm sorry" or "I feel bad that . . ." or starting a statement of our opinion with "I might be wrong, but . . ." We say it to the waitress when *she* screws up our order ("I'm sorry to bother you, but . . ."). We say it to our hairdresser when he gives us a cut we hate ("I feel bad telling you this, but . . ."). We say it to our date when the movie was bad ("I'm sorry you didn't like it, but the reviews . . ."). The list goes on and on. We're always apologizing, and even when we have absolutely nothing to apologize for, we still apologize: we apologize for not *anticipating* a problem, for not *avoiding* a problem, or for not *repairing* a problem. We apologize for what we do or say, or even who we are. I bet if you wrote down every time you said "I'm sorry" for a week, the number of times you actually said it would floor you. And add to that, the times you say "I'm sorry" indirectly. We don't always have to flat out say "I'm sorry" to apologize. We can apologize with the tone of our voice, by ending sentences with a question, and by not speaking up.

But it's time to stop saying "sorry." Especially for being single. Blaming yourself for being single is adding insult to injury. It's affecting the way you feel about yourself. And it's affecting the way you behave with men. The way you treat yourself isn't the result of your self-esteem. Your self-esteem is the result of the way you treat yourself. So start treating yourself with the esteem due to someone who's perfectly lovable.

> Krista, an RN at a busy Manhattan hospital, was dating Sam, a firefighter whom she really thought she might marry. She was always trying hard to please him, bending herself into pretzel-like contortions to be the woman she thought he wanted and apologizing profusely should anything go wrong in her perfectly organized plan. She thought Sam liked a woman who was the life of the party, because when they first met Krista had been the center of attention at a hospital holiday party she was hosting. So once they started dating, she made sure they were often part of a big group, like at a summer share house in the Hamptons or at

> a weekly poker party, even though she secretly wished they could spend more time alone. When her supervisor asked her to pick up extra shifts, Krista hesitated because she thought Sam would be upset. When she took the overtime, she called Sam and told him she was sorry for letting him down. When they finally talked it out, Sam said that he, of all people, knew what it was like to work long, hectic hours and she didn't have to apologize for it. He also said that he was tired of the whole party scene and wanted more time alone with her. Krista's first reaction was to begin to apologize to Sam for misreading him, but then she stopped herself. Her second reaction was better. She gave him a kiss and said, "Great!"

Krista still tried to please, but she asked before she put in effort, stopped apologizing when she fell short, and added herself to her list of those she was trying to please. And here's the best part: The more she pleased herself, the more Sam knew what pleased her. And tried to do the same.

It's time to stop saying "sorry." You're perfectly lovable as is—no ifs, ands, or buts. You're lovable no matter how much you weigh or what you ordered. You're lovable if you're wearing last year's fashions or if you're up on every trend. You're lovable if you'd rather spend the afternoon reading *People* than reading the *New York Times* or if you eat carbs instead of piling on the protein.

> Merri had a Brooklyn accent, and her Los Angeles friends mimicked her. She had bigger thighs than any other female public relations intern at the movie studio—maybe bigger than those of any twenty-three-year-old woman in all of California, she thought. She wasn't fat, she knew, and never felt fat before moving to the West Coast two years ago, but Merri knew that the micromini and bikinis were not for her. And her hair was brown, not blond. Reddish-brown and full—but not blond. Chris seemed to want to hang out with her anyway. She was booking his media tour for the action film he just starred in, and he could have told her to speak to his manager, but he didn't. She didn't understand it. He went over his itinerary with her over lunches, then dinners, and then he asked the studio to send her with him on his tour. When she would joke about her butt or Brooklyn accent or brown hair, he said, "Stop putting yourself down—it gives others ideas." She knew he was right. She stopped. They had fun traveling together. They're still together.

Don't Apologize for Being Single

Isn't it funny that when you're single, everyone from your dad to your dentist to your dry cleaner thinks it's all right to ask you *why* you're not part of a pair? Suddenly your love life is fair game and open to as much prodding and prying as people want to do. Your Uncle Joe screams across the Thanksgiving table that he thought you'd bring a date this year; your best friend's mom gives you that look of pity as she asks you, "Is it *that* hard to find a guy?"; and even the receptionist at your office feels justified in asking you why you don't just settle down. Don't apologize.

Rx: See being single as a fact, not a fault.

You don't owe anyone an explanation. Apologizing—giving an explanation—sends the message that it's okay to dig into your love life. It's *not* okay. Give the questioners details about your dating life and you're inviting them to make it their business. Plus, these kinds of questions just make you feel worse about yourself and make you forget how lovable you are as is. Soon you begin to feel as if maybe something *is* wrong with you because you didn't bring a guy to Thanksgiving or because you haven't met anyone yet. Then your self-esteem takes a nosedive and meeting someone becomes twice as difficult. When they ask, you have a lot of options:

Try changing the subject without any emotion

For example, when your aunt says, "You still haven't met a guy?" you can answer with, "No, but wait till you hear about the big promotion I got, sweater I made, melon I bought, trip I took, etc." You get the point. Casually switch the topic to something you *do* want to talk about. This tells her that you're happy with who you are, that being single isn't as big a deal to you as it obviously is to them, that you have other interests, and that your life isn't one big manhunt.

Try embracing the subject with overwhelming emotion

For example, when your dental hygienist asks you about your love life in front of the dental assistant, secretary, dentist's new wife (doing the billing, of course), and what seems like hundreds of other patients, work up a small catch in your throat, look down as if you're trying not to cry, and just shake your head from side to side instead of talking. If she has a brain and a heart, she'll never ask you again—particularly if you keep this act up for a while.

Try "joining the resistance"

For example, when your neighbor starts telling you how important it is to find a guy before you're too set in your ways, join her song and dance and outdo her. Agree with everything she says and add three more reasons that she's right. Tell her she doesn't know the half of it. Give her horror stories of women who didn't settle and therefore didn't settle down. It's a useful technique. If *you* tell *her* everything she's about to tell you—and more—what's left for *her* to say?

Don't Apologize to Friends

Sometimes friends offer to set you up and mean it when they say it but then let it slide. Don't say, "Sorry to be a pain, but you said you'd hook me up with your cute cousin." Don't apologize. She offered in the first place. Just remind her. Even though you know that your dating life isn't at the top of her to-do list and don't expect it to be, if she needs a nudge, give it to her.

And if a date's a bust, don't apologize to your friend who set you up for not liking the guy. You're entitled to like anyone you like, date who you want to date, and not date who you don't want to date, too. Don't spend one more minute than you have to with him just because you feel bad or are worried about her feelings. Even if nothing is outwardly wrong but you just have a vibe, trust your gut and your internal radar. It could be her best friend, her boss, her brother—it doesn't matter. They'll both get over it.

If the date's not a bust but a bonanza and you start dating someone, don't apologize to your friends for spending time with him. No, you shouldn't ditch them completely or give up girls' night out. But don't feel guilty or apologize because you're dating someone and they may not be. Life's a seesaw for everyone. Soon they'll be up again. Hopefully you won't be down.

Don't Apologize to Your Dates

If a guy asks you why you're still thirty-five and single, don't become defensive, defiant, or depressed. Don't give him a blow-by-blow description of your love life over the last few years or any details about past relationships—whether you've had them or not. Keep some of yourself under wraps, even if he asks. Just smile serenely and remember that you don't have to lay it all on the line on the first date or even the tenth. Leave him longing for more. If he likes you, and you like him, you'll see each other again and again and you can let it come out naturally. If, on the other hand, he thinks it's a big deal that you're thirty-five and single, you may want to rethink the guy. After all, if he's out with you, he's probably at least thirty-five and single too! Men don't apologize for anything. They don't apologize for being overweight or balding, dressing like a slob, or being single. Take note and take a lesson.

Don't apologize to him for not liking him, either. Once the date ends, you have every right to say "bye" and leave it there. If he calls for another date and you're not interested—no explanation or long speech about how sorry you are, how bad you feel, or how you're already involved with another man. It's not necessary. You're entitled to your feelings about him. Trust me, if the tables were turned, he'd say a nice good-bye and disappear—poof.

Most of All, Don't Apologize for Who You Are

Often those same people who feel compelled to query you about your single status are also nosy enough to tell you that if you just lost weight, worked less, were more assertive, cut your hair, and went to museums, you wouldn't be single. That's when you remind yourself to assume you're perfect just as you are. Don't change a thing. By changing who we are for others, we're apologizing for who we *really* are. We're saying, "You're right. I'm not good enough with this haircut, job, body, etc. I'm going to change for you." If you do, then you're not really you, and how long can you keep that up? The truth is that there are plenty of women with perfect bodies, cute haircuts, and lots of free time who are still single. There's nothing wrong with you and nothing about you that you should change just to meet a guy. If you love who you are and are happy with yourself, then don't change a thing.

> Ellen is one of those girls who everyone says has "such a pretty face" and would "be a knockout if she just lost some weight." They said that if Ellen lost some weight she'd "have guys falling at her feet." She heard that so many times that she believed it. So she lost twenty-five pounds. She looked thin. But guys weren't falling at her feet. Instead of feeling fabulous, she felt annoyed and frustrated. She also felt gullible. Soon she put ten pounds back on, by choice. She liked the way she looked—she looked like her. She never wanted to look skinny again. She ruled out any guy who let her know that he liked skinny, and then found a slim guy who loved her look.

At first, Ellen was dieting for guys she hadn't even met yet—and when she didn't meet them after all, she felt deprived. She felt deprived of food *and* deprived of her dream. In other words, she wasn't losing weight for herself. She was trying to change her body and become the "knockout" other people wanted her to be. She was apologizing to them for who she was by listening to them and gorging on grapefruits or cabbage soup to slim down. That's why so many people fail on diets. They're not changing their eating for themselves. To lose weight successfully, you have to feel as though you're giving yourself something (a healthier body), not depriving yourself of something (food, food, food).

Other people don't have the secret key to your life. Even if they could change you into their perfect version of you, there would be something even they can't control: him! Let them have their opinions. Let yourself have your own.

5 It's a Numbers Game

Here's another reason not to apologize for being single: It's not you, it's the statistics!

- The number of American singles has *jumped* recently, and almost 40 percent of American men and women are now unmarried, up from 28 percent one generation ago.
- The percentage of women twenty to twenty-four years old who hadn't married more than *doubled* between 1970 and 2003 (from 36 to 75 percent).
- Among women thirty to thirty-four years old, the pro-

portion who had still not married more than *tripled* since 1970 (from 6 to 23 percent).

- In 2003, the percentage of women currently married was 52, *down* from 60 percent in 1970.

So you're not alone in being single. You're part of a huge trend of Americans marrying later and later in life.

Now here's the good news:

- The *majority* of women in 2003 were married by the time they were thirty to thirty-four years old (72 percent)!
- Among men and women sixty-five years old and over, 96 *percent had been married* at some time.
- More men than women *stay single longer*, according to 2002 census data.
- About 62 percent of men in the prime dating ages of eighteen to thirty-four are still unmarried and *available* (compared to 51 percent of women).

And here's even more good news: More women today are marrying *younger* men than ever before in history. And there are more *young single men* to meet than in the 1970s—a big point in your favor. Then there are the men in the thirty-five to fifty age group. Many married young but threw themselves into their careers while their wives raised the children. Now their wives want their life back and the men want to have a family. Their wives move on. The men are *looking for a new family*. Another point in your favor. And finally there are the older men—fifty and up. Many are young at heart, young in spirit, and even young physically. *Most want to remarry* and want to remarry younger women. If you're over thirty-five yourself, they are probably about your age in maturity anyway.

In other words, overwhelmingly, *women will marry if they want to.* It just might take a while to find Mr. Right in a world of fixer-uppers. Bottom line: It's a numbers game. You don't know whether you'll be part of the 72 percent married by thirty-four or if you'll wait until forty-two with the clock ticking so loud you can't hear yourself think. It's not you . . . it's the times. Don't take it personally . . . just keep looking.

It's a Numbers Game—and the Odds Are on Your Side

Erin couldn't believe what her older brother was saying to her. She had been enjoying Thanksgiving dinner at his house, but now she was in shock. Her brother had called her into the study, asked her to sit down, and then suggested that she consider moving from Vermont to Alaska. "Why?" she asked, thinking at first that he was kidding. "Because you need a husband and there are so many more men than women in Alaska," he answered, completely serious. "I just saw the population numbers in *Newsweek*," he said, "and finding a husband is all a numbers game, you know." "So you think I'm such a hopeless case that I can't find a man to love me

> here? You think the odds I need are ten desperate, lonely men to every one woman?" "No," said her brother. "I think you're perfectly wonderful. But when I ask you about men, *you* sound hopeless and act as if *you* think you need those odds. Maybe you need ten times more men to find someone who *you* would marry."

Erin was stunned. Was she really sounding so hopeless? Had she really given up? She had to be honest with herself and say, "Could be." Her brother's talk was like shock therapy. No, she didn't move to Alaska, but she did decide that she would behave as if she had.

Erin chose to think of the pool of potential partners in Vermont as huge instead of small. That gave her hope. She chose to think of the guys in the pool as lonely and anxious to find a partner. That gave her courage. And she chose to think of her mission as finding just one lovable guy who finds her lovable, too. That gave her heart. The following Thanksgiving, she called her brother into the study and said, "Thank you."

Knowing That the Odds Are on Your Side Should Give You Heart, Too

But if you want to make sure you'll find a winner, make sure there are enough guys in the contest.

So often, the only difference between the woman with the man and woman still looking is that the married woman made sure to meet more men. Ask the married women you know how they met their husbands and learn flexibility from them. Don't rule out men with less education—they may have an attention deficit disorder but are geniuses at programming or picking stocks—and are more fun than a college professor. Don't rule out college professors, either, even if you didn't go to school one day past high school. They may love to show off to you, respect your hard work in the "real" world, and feel relieved that they don't have to compete with you in their own arenas.

Then rethink that tendency we have to look for guys who earn more than we do or have more status. It's dated. Women have made huge strides in the past fifteen years and have had time as singles to develop a career, raise their income, work overtime, and even buy a house. In fact, according to census statistics, single women own more than 14 million homes, more than double the number twenty-five years ago. That means almost one in every four homeowners is a single women (single men own only 12.6 percent), and it's not just because of inheritance or the spoils of divorce. We outpace men as new-home buyers, too, even though our average income is still lower. We don't really need to be taken care of like we used to, so why look only for men that can do that?

And as for those men in their late thirties and forties who have never married—suspend the suspicion long enough to see if your worst fears are true. (You wouldn't be as judgmental of an unmarried woman the same age!) In other words, stop setting up artificial barriers before a relationship even begins. Throw out your categories and look at each guy as an individual. He might be shy, not gay. He might be slow to mature, paying back loans, self-conscious about his sexual performance, afraid of being hurt, worried about supporting a family or raising children. It's a numbers game, and all you need is one. Keep your numbers big.

Don't Confuse Men with Women

That's right. Most of all, don't confuse men with women. Many of us do. We say we want to meet only someone with sympathy, sensitivity, and a sense of humor, who likes to talk, touch, and try new experiences. We want someone who will empathize, and anticipate. Who will apologize on his own. Who will remember our birthday, our advice, and our anxieties.

We're describing our girlfriends! Our mothers! Ourselves! Forget it. That ideal androgynous he-male doesn't exist. If he did, he'd be *perfect*—a man with all our best female traits and his own manly sex appeal, too—but *there are no perfect men*. So stop confusing men with women, or you'll be ruling everyone out.

> Lily broke up with Adam because he bought her an ornate hand-carved mahogany jewelry box for her birthday. "It's not me," she told everyone. "If he could think this is my taste, then he just doesn't know me. If this is *his* taste, I don't want to know him!" Next she broke up with Patrick because he

> didn't think the movies *Closer* and *Million Dollar Baby* were sad. "He thought those movies were just good stories," she told her sister. "He didn't get the metaphor, the meaning, or the message," she said. "So?" replied her sister. "So he's not for me," Lily answered; "I need someone I can talk to." "Talk to *me*," said her younger, but wiser, sister. But Lily ruled Patrick out. And then she ruled Seth out, too, because he didn't offer to go with her to her great-aunt's wake—she had to ask.

Lily was looking for a guy who was her alter ego, a perfect fit, a guy who was just like her. Her younger sister, on the other hand, was looking for a guy who's perfectly lovable instead of perfect. She's now married. Lily isn't.

Rx: Look for a guy who's perfectly lovable instead of perfect. That's the one way a guy really can be just like us.

Of course there are men who are not living stereotypes. Many spend less time developing their careers, for example, than their relationships with their family or friends, both men and women. But that doesn't mean that they do it *our* way. Most still do it *their* way. Less talking and more walking. Sharing stories and beers instead of feelings and tears. Don't throw *them* out of the game, either. They may call home a lot and seem to be mama's boys, but maybe they just love their mothers. They may spend less time at the office and seem to be underachievers, but maybe they just define success differently. They may not dazzle your parents or seem "good enough" to your friends, but in the end, your friends and your parents have their own lives—this is yours.

6 Lose the List

Ask almost any woman about the kind of guy she wants to meet and she can rattle off a mental checklist of must-have details about her ideal man, from the color of his eyes to his occupation. This résumé of required traits is what we call our "type," and we often spend all our dating years looking for him, dating him, and steering clear of guys who don't measure up. But you're still single. Maybe it's because your type isn't the only guy for you. Maybe your type isn't your type at all.

> By the time Gerri was a teenager, she'd had her perfect man all picked out. He'd be tall—six feet at

> least. He'd have lots of hair—blondish. He'd have a great sense of humor and would love her sense of humor, too. In fact, he'd hang on every word and have eyes only for her. Of course, he'd have a great job and make plenty of money, and love to surprise her—especially with expensive jewelry and romantic weekend getaways.

Do I need to tell you that Gerri never did find a guy who met all those qualifications? Are there any who could live up to them? Very few, that's for sure.

Gerri's problem was that she didn't remember all of the assumptions:

1. She definitely assumed she was perfectly lovable.

2. She also assumed that she was entitled, therefore, to a perfect man . . . (just like the one she'd always wanted).

But then she made some mistakes:

3. She assumed there are perfect men (there aren't, just perfectly lovable men).

4. She assumed, therefore, that every man she met could be the "perfect" one (on paper, that is).

As a result, Gerri was not only single but very discouraged. She wasn't even enjoying dating. Instead of seeing dates as interesting new people, she was so hung up on her "list" that if a guy didn't fit the bill—literally and figuratively—she passed him by. She rarely dated men who were of average or short height, and she almost never looked at a guy with a receding hairline. "He's not my type," she would say when her coworkers wondered why she wasn't interested in the cute guy in Finance who was a lot of fun but also slightly balding.

Gerri just wasn't the type of woman who could compromise when it came to men, she told herself. She thought she was taking care of herself and maximizing her chance of success. But she was setting herself up for failure, and you may be doing the same thing. By focusing on only one type—say, all the blond-haired, creative men who love the same hobbies you do, you're not only narrowing your preselection of available men but are also creating three more problems:

1. You'll have blinders on when you actually meet guys (admit it, you quickly compare them against the list, then discount them when they fall short).

2. You'll make it harder for your friends to introduce you to guys. When you constantly talk about your type to other people like friends or coworkers, their mental Rolodex of guys to set you up with shrinks.

3. You'll miss the crowd. The more detailed your checklist, or the more perfect a match you're trying to find

between the guys you meet and your checklist, the harder it is to find someone and the longer it will take. So what, you say? You're willing to wait? Here's the catch. Once you are out of school, once most of your friends are married, and once you've moved out of a community where everyone knows the background of the guys you're meeting, you're on your own. Trust me. It's easier to comb the woods in a group!

The "Unwritten List"

Even if we tell ourselves we don't have a "list," research finds we do have one. I call it our "unwritten list." From the time we're very young, the movies we see, the books we read, and the couples we know influence our attractions and infatuations. So does what we like about our father, grandfathers, brothers, uncles, teachers, doctors, and even schoolmates. And then there are all the universal traits that history tells us have seduced women for centuries—decisiveness and risk-taking mixed with tenderness and humor. And the traits that, according to polls, today's American women want:

A sense of humor (or at least the same sense of humor!)
Similar ideas about the future
Looks
Intelligence
Financial stability or good earning potential

Best friend qualities
Romantic behavior
A desire for a family
Sexual compatibility and sexual faithfulness
Willingness to share responsibilities

Add it all together and you've got a character from a romance novel. He's what we'd *all* create if we could create a mate, but we can't. We've got to work with what God created. And that's okay, because the same rule applies the other way around, too. When I say we are perfect as we are, and perfectly lovable as we are, I'm not saying we're all exactly what a guy would create if he could make *his* list come true. I'm saying we don't have to be! Just take a look at their list, according to polls. Men say they want women with the following traits:

Honesty
Attractiveness
Physical fitness
Intelligence
Sexual forwardness (but only with them)
Loving and nurturing personality
A good sense of humor (which means appreciative of *his* sense of humor)
An upbeat, not moody, disposition

Of course men want all that, but it's love, not a list, that makes them want to get married. They tell researchers they marry because they fall in love, like and want to be with a particular woman, want children, want to share responsibilities, and think married life is an easier life—in that order! So be yourself, and let them be themselves, too.

The Do-Over List

Without even realizing it, sometimes we look for someone today who is just like someone in our past, so we can have a "do-over." If that someone in our past was warm, loving, and supportive, it's a great idea—as long as you don't expect a clone. Look for the same qualities, not the identical personality. Remember, there is no perfect match. No "perfect" match for you, and no "perfect" match to anyone in your past, either.

Sometimes, however, that someone in our past was not very lovable but we find we're attracted to similar men anyway. For example, if we had a cold father, an aggressive brother, or a bullying family, we may be looking for someone similar and re-creating the same type of situation again in order to make it come out different this time. Sound like a good idea on paper? It's definitely *not* a good idea! Even if you win that cold guy over or placate the angry guy, you still have to deal with the original problem. A do-over isn't a makeover for your life. Accept that you had a bad situation that was beyond your control when you were young. Now use all your adult control to erase your unwritten list.

Getting Real

But a lot of women say, "My list is fine. It's not a do-over or makeover list. I'll be lowering my standards if I give it up." Actually, it's your *expectations* you'll probably be lowering, and if that means you'll be getting "real" instead of getting frustrated, so much the better. Women who hang on to romantic notions sometimes have "Cinderella complexes"—they're waiting for the handsome prince to rescue them from romance hell and change their lives. But the fantasy never comes true, because only *you* can change your life. And here's how you can do it. Trade your list of fantasies for my list of realities. Specifically:

Assume that there is a more perfect match for you than the man you're dating, somewhere in the world.

Assume, however, that if it took you many years to find the imperfect guy you're now dating, it may take you just as many years or more to find a better one.

Now, do you still want to throw him away and stick to your list?

Getting real means understanding that men are real, not ideal. Perfectly lovable, never perfect. Sure, if you could build a boyfriend, then, yes, you could come up with this ideal man. But you can't build a boyfriend (at least not yet), and it's not lowering your standards to accept this and focus on who he is, not whom you want him to be. Take Melissa.

Melissa's list read like this: her guy must be athletic, the same age as she, from a close-knit Jewish family, and a lawyer or other suit-wearing business type, with dark hair and dark eyes. Almost every guy she dated fit this description, yet the relationships never went too far. Then she met Jake. Fifteen years her senior, he was an artist who wore paint-splattered pants. Plus, he was Catholic, and had a receding hairline (though the strands he *did* have were brown). He hardly spoke to his parents, who lived three thousand miles away. Melissa and Jake connected instantly. After just a few casual conversations, she had this amazing feeling that she'd known him forever. Though their bond intensified over the next few months and they were obviously a couple, Melissa denied—to herself—that this guy was The One. Nothing about him lined up with her checklist, so how *could* he be The One? She didn't even introduce him to her parents for six months because she thought, *He's not my type, so we won't be together that long*. Still, months went by. The relationship got more serious. Then one of her friends said, "You're going to marry this guy." It stunned her, but she knew her friend was right. She realized her last boyfriend had been her type to a T, and he bored her to tears. She realized that being connected and happy with someone was more important than his age, height, or income bracket.

The lesson here? You may actually bond with someone who doesn't have your required résumé. Of course, there are things you don't have to bend on, like wanting him to be honest or have an interest in having a family. But pick which traits you *must* have, then let the others be a surprise. There isn't just one type of guy who is going to find *you* perfectly lovable. There are lots! So there are probably many types out there who would totally turn you on that you don't even know exist.

Think of it like this: It's like eating only chocolate chip ice cream your whole life. Yes, you love vanilla ice cream, you love chocolate chips, and it's delicious and satisfying. But maybe there's another flavor out there—say, cookie dough—that you've never tried: maybe one you don't know about but would love as much or more if only you just tasted it.

Rx: Open yourself up to new possibilities by ordering from a different love menu.

So, here's your assignment. This month, give at least two different types of guys a chance, and stop saying "He's not my type." Maybe you like artsy men but your friend's preppy cousin asks you out. Go for it. It's just a date. Remind yourself of all those perfect-on-paper guys who bored you silly or broke your heart.

You've spent your whole life dating one type, so now try

some others. And be positive about it. Tell yourself you're taking a chance on love. If you focus on your list and what he's lacking, any date will feel your disappointment when he falls short.

Rx: If dating your type were the key to romance, then you wouldn't still be single.

Of course, in the end, you may wind up with a guy who has lots of traits from your checklist, and that's fine. But then again, you might not. Don't think of it as settling if you fall in love with someone who doesn't fit the list. If he makes your heart skip a few beats and finds you perfectly lovable, that's far from settling. That's a happy ending.

Opposites Can Attract

Remember to stop the "all or nothing" point of view we spoke about, too. For example, don't automatically say no to a date with a guy who happens to be younger than you. Younger women have been dating older men for years, and now women are finding that it's just as acceptable, even chic, to date younger men. If it works for Demi Moore, why shouldn't it work for you?

You should also be open to dating a man who may be in a different income tax bracket, too, if you're attracted to him. Some women, like Kristin, a lawyer, don't like to go out with men who aren't professionals, too. But they are cutting themselves off from a whole sea of men who may not have gone to college or grad school but still make a good living. What matters is whether you have a connection. That's what happened to Marie, a teacher with a master's degree who ended up marrying an electrician with a high school diploma. Besides, in many areas of the country, a skilled union worker like an electrician can make more money than many men with so-called professional jobs.

Religion may be a trickier one to navigate, especially if your romance turns serious. One woman I know will not even date non-Jewish men because she knows she will never marry someone who is not of her faith. That may sound extreme, especially when it seems that the relationship will never go beyond the dating stage. But it worked for Rebecca because she felt she didn't want to lead anyone on or get her own heart broken. On the other hand, many mixed-faith marriages are successful, and in other cases women or men convert to the religion of their loved ones, like Charlotte, the WASP socialite in *Sex and the City*, who became Jewish for her soul mate.

Rx: Be open-minded about differences. There's a reason they say opposites attract.

Only you know what works for you, especially when it comes to something as intensely personal as religion. But don't *automatically* shut yourself off from someone just because on the face of it he's different from you.

Toss Other People's Checklists

Even if you decide to lose your list, your friends and family probably still have one for you—and your mother's is usually a whole lot longer than yours was! She may not tell you flat out, but she's got a picture of her future son-in-law perfectly painted in her head. The problem? He's just in her mind. Her perfect guy doesn't exist any more than your perfect guy did. So if you hear your mother's voice, or your best friend's, or whoever's in your head when a guy who's not her type asks you out, tell that voice to be quiet, and then go for it. You just never know.

Maybe you've passed up a perfectly datable guy because you were worried about what your friends would think and then regretted it when he started dating one of your friends. Or took a pass because you thought a guy wasn't up to your best friend's boyfriend's standards, and then kicked yourself when you saw who her boyfriend hangs out with.

If you worry too much about fulfilling others' expectations or impressing your friends or family, you can easily let a really great guy slip away. And, in the end, if you find a guy who treats you right and makes you happy, they'll probably be happy too—whether he's their type or not.

Chuck the Couple Checklist, Too

Let's say you've done it. You've found a lovable guy who finds you perfectly lovable, too. Once it's clear that the two of you are a couple and might actually be going somewhere, don't be like many women and pull out list number two: details about everything a perfect relationship should be. The inevitable result is that you start questioning if he's The One because you run down this checklist of what should or shouldn't happen in a perfect relationship, and things don't ever line up for long. You think, *If he were really The One, he'd always be able to read my mind, we'd have earth-shattering sex every time, or we'd never argue*. Wrong! Maybe that kind of couple exists in the movies, but this isn't the big screen. This is real life, not reel life. Find me a couple that doesn't irritate each other or argue at least once in a while. They just don't exist.

Rx: When it comes to men, take yourself off automatic pilot and choose your course.

Forget the myth of the Perfect Couple. You're not going to always be able to read each other's minds, get along, and be perfectly in sync in bed. You're not going to want to spent 24/7 together, he's not always going to buy you the perfect birthday gift, and at times his little habits are going to bug you (and vice versa). No pair is perfect. Not your parents, not your best friend and her man, and certainly not your favorite celebrity couple (look at what happened to Brad and Jen).

You may see relationships that seem ideal, but you're on the outside looking in. No matter how close you are to your friend or sister, you can't know all of what goes on behind closed doors. You think your friend's boyfriend is beyond great, but after they break up your friend may tell you he was moody, uptight, and lazy in bed. Let's face it: Lots of men "show" well.

Even life with Mr. Right can become routine—that's normal and shows a comfort level that you've attained. It shows that you can be you. Isn't it funny that when we're single we want a guy we're comfortable with, one with whom we can stay home on a Friday night while wearing sweatpants, watching a movie, and ordering in Chinese food, but when we finally get that guy and that relationship, we worry that it's routine. It's not; it's reality.

When you do decide to be in a relationship with a guy, give it a chance. Stop wondering what else is out there or thinking *I should have, could have, would have*. Again, remember these basics:

Assume there is a more perfect match for you than the man you're dating, somewhere in the world.

Assume, however, that if it took you many years to find the imperfect guy you're now dating, it may take you just as many years or more to find a better one.

There's also the chance, of course, that you'll never find a better one—just a different one.

Rx: Trade the myth of perfection for the math of probabilities.

A perfect match doesn't exist; the man who loves you does.

7 Meet Him Halfway

Given that no man is perfect, it is our duty to be compassionate. If he's so imperfect that he does not find us lovable, then we say a nice good-bye. If he does find us lovable, on the other hand, or it's too soon to tell if he might, we must be generous and meet him halfway.

It could be as simple as where you go for dinner. You may think a first date at a diner is wildly inappropriate because you'll spend half the time looking at the lettuce stuck in his teeth. But don't turn down his suggestion immediately. If he wants to show you the best homemade food place in town, let him. Sometimes he's picking a place where he's comfortable, or known. Sometimes he's trying to lower your expectations so he won't feel as if he can't top himself on the next date. Sometimes it's a really special place but you've never heard of it. (Unless you write for *Zagats*, you can't know all the hot spots.) Take Beth, for example.

> A guy Beth met through work and had been flirting with for weeks finally asked her out. She lived in suburbia and he lived in the city, but they definitely had a connection when they spoke on the phone. He invited her to dinner where he lived. She was thrilled. She spent hours getting ready, picking out her outfit and daydreaming about their romantic night on the town. She slipped on her favorite dress, fancy earrings, and even had her hair done. You can imagine her surprise, then, when he picked her up and drove her to a pizza place for dinner. A pizza place! A pizza place where you don't make a reservation but wait in line outside until they scream your name. A pizza place with paper tablecloths and sticky plastic cups. A pizza place where they shuffled customers in and out like a herd of cows. There was Beth in her finest clothes, perfect makeup, and good jewelry, sweating as she sat only five feet from a scorching brick oven, with potbellied men tossing dough into the air and cursing in Italian. She was horrified and couldn't wait for the date to be over. *He must not think much of me if he took me to a place like that on our first date,*

she thought, and she never gave him a second glance or returned his phone calls after that.

It was only a few years later that she realized that he had taken her to the number one pizza place in New York City. One that was famous worldwide for its thin-crust pizza. One where people came from all over just to squeeze into one of those booths and sweat by those brick ovens. One where the rich and famous were willing to stand in line outside just to get a slice.

The moral of the story is probably obvious. Don't judge a book by its cover. Don't judge a date or a restaurant or your guy's plans or lack of plans. Sometimes it's too early for you to know the meaning behind a place or plan he has for your first date. And yes, sometimes it's just a bad choice and many times you will know better, but remember—he's imperfect and you must act with compassion and generosity. You never know, you may wind up together and laugh about it later.

It's important to be flexible in a relationship, especially at the beginning, when you're just getting to know each other. Try looking at things from his perspective. You thought he was boring and couldn't hold a conversation. Maybe he was just nervous and tongue-tied. Maybe he realized that the pizza joint wasn't the best choice of a restaurant for a first date and was embarrassed and worried about your reaction. Remember to assume that *everything he may say and do is information about him, not you.*

Maybe you're saying, wait a minute! What about zero

tolerance when you're getting zero? But this is not about getting zero. Zero tolerance doesn't mean loving only a perfect man (there's no such thing!); it is about leaving a man who doesn't love you. When a man loves you, or you think he might love you soon, compassion and generosity only make love grow.

Besides, if you meet him halfway, chances are you'll have more fun. Why? Because you've agreed to share control of the situation. Instead of feeling uptight because you took full responsibility for making the date special, or gave up all the responsibility and had no choice at all, you can both relax and enjoy the evening. Even if the restaurant really didn't deserve that four-star review or the movie you saw should have received a big thumbs down, no one is to blame—you were in it together.

Rx: Take 50 percent of the chances and make 50 percent of the choices in a relationship, and you'll be giving it 100 percent of a try.

Some books about dating will tell you to let your man take the lead, that he will love you only if he has to hunt you like prey. But in real life you've probably noticed that your married friends met more casually. They were friends first, or they met at work and they drifted into love, with a little effort on both sides.

Halfway vs. No Way

Since there's no such thing as a perfect man, there are lots of things you have to be willing to accept for now, just to get things going. *Then* you can decide if he's for you, but at first give it time.

Take how he dresses, for example. In the beginning it's hard to look past someone's appearance because it's all you've go to go on. But it's just too easy to notice his J Crew pants and cable-knit sweater and discount him because he wouldn't go with your trendy Manolo Blahniks. Give him a chance and ignore the outfit. Look inside the clothes (figuratively speaking, of course!). Don't discount him because his style doesn't mesh with yours. Think about it. If you heard that a guy didn't call you for another date just because he didn't like your sense of fashion, you'd think he was a total jerk. Well, don't be the jerk.

Don't brush off his interests, either. No, you don't have to memorize the names and numbers of his favorite football team. You don't even have to know the name of the team. But once in a while you can meet him halfway and go to a game with him or grab some burgers and beers at a sports bar. Give it a chance. First of all, you never know. You actually may like it. It's something new, something you've never done, so approach it with an open mind. But even if you hate it, giving it a chance, meeting him halfway in terms of his interest, says a lot about you to him. I'm not suggesting that you feign interest in say, hiking, if you hate it. But giving it a try or doing it every once in a while shows him that you care enough about him to learn more about the things he likes, you want to know what makes him tick, and you care about him. He'll be touched. He also may do the same for you and meet you halfway with your interests. It's worth it.

Meet him halfway if you're traveling together. Your idea of the perfect vacation may be lying on the beach, sipping a margarita, and catching up on your favorite book or magazines. He may be the active type who enjoys scuba diving, water skiing, and parasailing. A great compromise could be an all-inclusive resort where you both get what you want. But if you really want to meet him halfway, get up off your lounge chair a few times and go with him on his adventures. You may not be up for scuba diving, but maybe you can convince him to try snorkeling with you. One couple I know plans trips to Florida during baseball's spring training season. They split their time between the beach and other attractions while keeping a few days free for a game.

Meet him halfway when it comes to his friends. His friends may be a bunch of obnoxious guys or simply rub you the wrong way, but don't hold that against him. Let him have his time with his friends. Meet him halfway by not criticizing them or putting them down. You may not like them, but you don't have to go on and on about it. It's hurtful to him, and it may make him think twice about you. (Besides, if you're understanding about his friends, he's more likely to be tolerant and understanding of yours—even though I'm sure they're all great!) And once in a while, hang out with his pals, for his sake. Make the effort to be friendly with them, especially the women in the crowd.

That way you don't come off as an interloper: you start to be part of the group.

The same goes for his family. His mother may be an overbearing nightmare or his sister may be a total snob. But that doesn't mean he's not the one for you. Give them a chance for your relationship's sake. I know lots of women who met guys and loved their close-knit, involved families. Then time went on and they found that "involved" meant "nosy" and "close-knit" meant "overbearing." The longer you're dating someone and the closer you get, the closer you get to his or her family. You see beyond the initial facade and may not like what you find there. It works the other way, too. Once you get to know his family, you may actually find things you like.

Speaking of family and friends, there are times you'll just have to meet each other halfway by agreeing to ignore your respective loved ones and their opinions. Don't listen to the girlfriends who ask what you, the literary one in the group, see in your guy, whose idea of leisure reading is *Sports Illustrated*. Don't listen to your parents, who wonder why you're dating a construction supervisor instead of the doctor you used to see. If the two of you are happy, then make a pact to shut out the naysayers and enjoy being together. In the end, your differences might split you apart. But it will have been your decision, not because you caved in to peer pressure. You're not in high school anymore and you can date whomever you want if it makes you happy.

Agree to Disagree

Sociologists say that the one absolute necessity for any group to survive is this: agreement about what to do when they disagree. The same is true for any couple, and the best strategy is to meet halfway and agree to disagree. That means if you're out on a first or second or early date and you hit on a topic that you totally disagree about, just agree to disagree instead of turning the date into a debate. Or stop arguing your position and try to see things from his point of view just to learn more about the other side of the issue. Or point out where you *do* have similarities, because no matter how firm people's stances are there are always gray areas.

Sure, it may signal that you're not meant to be together since you're so opposite, but then again, opposites can attract—if they agree on even bigger issues like faith and family. (Think Maria Shriver and Arnold Schwarzenegger or Mary Matalin and James Carville.) Eventually, if the two of you end up in a long-term relationship and everything else is great but you can't agree on politics, you'll either make a rule that you don't talk about that subject and agree to respect each other's point of view, or you'll debate it if that kind of feisty banter is one of the things that you both like in your relationship.

Tell Him What You Want

You're also more likely to get what you want if you tell him what you want. Women are good mind readers. We put ourselves in others' positions, empathize with their feelings, and anticipate their needs. Men are usually not good mind readers. Studies say they assume everyone is in the same position as they are, they sympathize but don't empathize with others' feelings, and they are surprised by others' needs. So make his life easier—talk to him. If something is bothering you, tell him—and try to help him see what you're saying.

If you think relationships should be easier than this, that communication should be automatic, and that meeting halfway means you're going out of your way, think again. We don't expect our friends to be our cosmic clones or even our family to be perfectly in tune with us, so why expect such complete compatibility from a guy we just met?

Rx: Compromising doesn't mean giving in or giving up. It just means giving.

Give your dates and mates some of the same patience and flexibility you show even your casual acquaintances, and you'll be giving love a chance.

8 With Mr. Big, Timing Is Everything

Sometimes the only thing wrong with a "perfect" man—the one who matches everything on your list—is that he doesn't want to marry you. But that's the biggest imperfection of all. If he's not ready to be with you, then he's not the perfect guy. Not now. Maybe not ever. Don't wait. Don't try to change his mind. Let him go. You need to spend your time looking for someone who thinks you're perfectly lovable—and who is ready to commit to you.

I know it's hard to accept, but if the timing is bad, there's nothing you can do to change the eventual outcome. Timing is something we can't control, and of course as women that drives us crazy. We're used to fixing things. We're good at figuring out what's wrong and making it better. Just tell us what's troubling you, and we'll try to find a solution. So of course we try to fix the timing problem, too. But it's *his* problem, and only time can fix it.

To gain some sense of control over the situation, we usually blame ourselves. We convince ourselves that timing wouldn't count if he was really "in love." And why wasn't he really "in love"? Because we weren't perfect enough. If it's our fault, then at least we have a prayer of correcting it. Does this sound familiar? "It was me! I nagged him too much" or "I was too jealous and it drove him away." In fact, we find it so hard to believe that something as intangible as bad timing could be the culprit that we tell each other that the "timing thing" is just a lame excuse used by a guy looking to dump someone. But it's not. Timing is real and it counts. He may not even be aware that the problem is timing, but if he doesn't feel as though he can move forward, there's nothing you can do to change his mind.

That's what happened to Theresa.

> When the man Theresa was dating for more than a year told her he wasn't ready and wanted his freedom, she was heartbroken. She really thought Mark was the one—he seemed so committed, loyal, and loving. In fact, she had told her family and friends that she could picture the two of them getting married. So not only was she upset about the breakup but she was embarrassed that she had misread his intentions and that he moved on immedi-

> ately. Her friends gave her a few months to grieve over the end of the relationship but got concerned when Theresa wouldn't let go of the fantasy of reuniting with Mark. "She just couldn't get it in her head that the timing wasn't right for her and Mark and that it was over for good," said her best friend, Jeanine. "I've tried fixing her up with guys from work. She's not interested. We've tried encouraging her to flirt with cute men we meet at clubs, and she doesn't even want to be there. It's time to move on, and she just can't stop fixating on Mark."

Theresa was forgetting the third assumption:

Assume that there is no perfect man . . . in the whole world, and every man you meet will be imperfect . . . in many ways.

Theresa wanted to see Mark as perfect, her only chance at true love. But there was no perfect Mark. The real Mark was not the guy she thought she was dating. Perfect Mark was loyal, committed, and loving. Real Mark wasn't ready, so he couldn't be loyal, committed, and loving. In fact, within a week, he was dating someone else. No man is perfect, of course, but Mark wasn't even perfectly lovable.

Theresa isn't alone. We've all done it—stayed in relationships too long, making excuses for his bad behavior, thinking he'll come around eventually. We think, *Okay, he doesn't want to marry me today, but he'll change his mind soon.* We're afraid that if we let go, we won't be in place to catch him when he is ready. But if the timing is off, trust me, it could be a long wait. At that point, you're just convenient to him, and that is no way to live or love.

Assume that if he doesn't find you lovable, that's proof that he's imperfect . . . at least for you.

If you don't, chances are he'll come to you one day and say, "I've met someone else." His timing may have finally improved and he's ready for a serious relationship, but not with you.

Rx: If the feelings aren't mutual, move on. If he misses you, he'll follow. If he doesn't, good riddance.

If he does follow, however, there's no guarantee that things will be different. He might now see *you* differently (as the love of his life, or someone essential to his emotional survival), but does he see *himself* differently as well? Does he now see himself as a grown-up, ready to start his own family, help to support a family, pledge sexual fidelity, and share decisions? If his view of himself hasn't changed, not much else will, either. Sometimes, even love is not enough. If he's not ready or steady, he'll still be dragging his feet even though absence made his heart grow fonder. It's not you, it's him. Unless you have time to wait, and waste, move on.

The Commitment Phobia Fallacy

When Theresa finally gave up on Mark, she told herself, and everyone else who would listen, that Mark was "commitment phobic." Technically, this means that making a long-term choice triggers feelings of panic and claustrophobia. Therefore, not only is making a decision difficult, but just the *anticipation* of making a decision can also produce the symptoms of anxiety. Men (and women) who truly suffer from this affliction spend most of their lives dithering when it's crunch time and avoiding any real responsibility for shaping their life. Even picking a car is a painful process filled with indecision and followed by buyer's remorse. Just imagine how difficult picking a spouse would be!

The truth is that most men (and women) who are single, even if they are older than thirty or forty, are *not* really commitment phobic. They typically have no problems making long-term commitments to their families, their career, their friends, and even their pets. They commit to playing on teams, joining clubs, helping their parents, being a godparent, or attending graduate school. They still call their grade school buddies, join the marines, and take twenty-year loans. They may be avoiding marriage, but not because they are incapable of making the decision or would suffer from panic attacks if they did. It's more likely to be immaturity, unrealistic expectations, reluctance to share, romantic notions, disinterest, or career concerns. In other words, just bad timing. And it doesn't really matter. Instead of figuring out fancy diagnoses, move on. If you convince yourself that he's commitment phobic, you're more likely to try to "help" him with his "problem" rather than helping yourself by looking somewhere else.

He's Baaaaack . . .

Occasionally, the stars will align and he becomes ready, like Marianne's boyfriend in Chapter 1. But there is no guarantee that when he is ready, he'll come back for *you*. So get back out there—even if it's just to prepare yourself for his return.

That's what Carrie did on *Sex and the City*. She carried a torch for Mr. Big for many years but still dated others because Big couldn't commit to her. As most of you know, that story had a happy ending: Big realized Carrie was the one and decided to move back to Manhattan to be with her. Their timing was finally right. Here's the thing, though—as she continued to date others, Carrie learned in the end that he really was the man for her. So it's never a waste of time to see other men; it's all information you can use.

9 There's No Such Thing as "Just Friends"

Think about the most perfect man you know. Not Orlando Bloom or Will Smith. I mean a man you really know. Someone with whom you've gone to the movies, had lunch, fought and laughed with. Very often women tell me the most perfect man they know is "just a friend." Sometimes he's a woman's "best friend."

> Since law school, Lauren and Justin were pals. They went to movies together, pigged out most Sunday nights, and took each other to their office parties whenever they needed to make a good impression.

> Lauren was critical of most of the men she was meeting, but not of Justin. Sure, she knew he just seemed more perfect than blind dates because she cut him more slack, forgave more, and expected less—after all, she wasn't measuring him for lifelong wear. But when she tried to set him up with one of her friends and recited his virtues, she had to admit he really was pretty impressive, even by objective standards. *Maybe*, she thought, *I'm so critical of other guys because I measure them against Justin*. She wondered if things would have been different if they had met on a date, and she wondered if Justin ever wondered, too. *I wonder*, she thought, *if there's such a thing as "just friends."*

Does this sound familiar? It should, because the odds are that you are one of the many women who have a man in their lives who's a "best friend." If you do, that's great. If you don't, see if you can find one, for a few reasons:

1. First, you can practice your new approach on him

From now on, assume you're perfect when you talk to him. Stop complaining about yourself to him. Stop blaming yourself for being single when you talk to him. Stop asking him for advice about men—perfect women are perfectly lovable and don't need makeovers from men, not even men who are their best friends. Besides, most men aren't very good at emotional advice, anyway. They take each other, and us, at face value—as package deals. That's why it's so easy to be with a man who's "just a friend." In fact, you're happy that he doesn't notice your hair—you don't have to spend hours on it.

From now on, assume he's *not* perfect—or at least not as perfect as you've thought. That doesn't mean that you have to point out all his flaws to him or start a makeover on him. Just make sure you notice that his imperfections don't make him less lovable in your eyes. Then make sure you remember that any teeny-weeny imperfections you may have don't make you any less than perfectly lovable, either!

2. Next, you can practice being yourself with him

Since you are perfectly lovable as you are, you can be exactly who you are when you're with men. Try it out on him.

Pretend he's a date. Be you.
Pretend he's a blind date. Be you.
Pretend he's someone you're beginning to find fascinating. Be you.
Pretend he's someone who shares your interests and attitudes. Be you.
Picture him as someone you'd consider spending your life with. Be you.

3. Then, you can practice dating with him

Since you are perfectly lovable as you are, you can expect him to act as if you're lovable. See if he does. Watch him, not yourself.

Rx: Remember, on any date (real or practice), everything he may say and do is information about him, not you!

Pretend you're his date. Observe *him*.
Pretend you're his blind date. Observe *him*.
Pretend you're someone he's beginning to find fascinating. Observe *him*.
Pretend you're someone who shares his interests and attitudes. Observe *him*.
Picture yourself as someone he'd consider spending the rest of his life with. Observe *him*.

4. *Now you can take another look at him*

You may be surprised. After all that "practice" dating, you may find that he's the best real date you've had in a long time. And it makes sense, since he was prescreened by you! To become your friend, he first had to have a sense of humor and a capacity for empathy (just like your girlfriends)—the very same qualities we tell pollsters we want in a man!

Uncovering "Hidden Romance"

So here he is. An imperfect but great guy who can also be a best friend. Sounds great. What's the problem? Most of us want romance, too. We want to be swept off our feet, feel tingles when we're touched and thrills when we're kissed.

Just look at your friend as if you're meeting him for the

first time. Is he interesting, considerate, attentive, and amusing? Does he share your attitudes and values? Does he enjoy the things you enjoy? If the answer is yes, ask yourself how often this combination comes along. If you decide that it's not often, take a second look at your friend.

Look at your friend as if you're with him for the *last* time. Pretend he's met somebody who adores him and wants him all to herself. Pretend he's buying her gifts and making love to her. Pretend that since you're "just friends," he'll be moving on and will be saying good-bye. Are you just a little jealous? Are you just a little competitive? Are you just a little angry that she got him? Although you want him to be happy, do you feel that losing him will make you unhappy? If the answer is yes to any of these questions, you've got *hidden romance*—and it's time to uncover it.

> Lauren and Justin went to their fifth law school reunion together last spring and noticed that their friendship had already outlasted some of their classmates' marriages. They were being treated as a couple by their friends and began to feel like a couple that weekend. They were in a hotel, far from home, and alone together—and loved it. They are still together as more than friends.

Have you heard people say "there's no such thing as 'just friends' "? What they usually mean is one of the following:

1. That at least one member of that male-female relationship is probably "in love" with the other or the friend-

ship wouldn't have lasted. We're all so busy trying to find mates, get ahead, stay in touch with our girlfriends, visit our family, and stay fit, that "just friends" become "just history" unless there's something more there. Was there more there for Lauren and Justin all along? Justin says he was always a bit in love with Lauren, but Lauren says she doesn't really know.

2. That any man and woman can make sparks fly. That's what I meant by "hidden romance." It's human nature. We're built to fall in love. It's how nature encourages us to make a commitment and procreate. Put any man and woman on a desert island and see what happens. Put yourself and your "friend" on a psychological desert island and see what happens. Stop looking over every hill and around every corner for someone sexier or more mature or handsomer and take a good look at him. Stop comparing him to men you might never meet, and look at what you have. If there's a bit of a flutter, a touch of tingling, or even a warm flush starting, the hidden romance is coming out.

3. That it's a lot easier to add romance to a friendship than a friendship to a romance! Any two people can fall into bed, but most won't really fall in love—or even like each other in the morning. Imagine how great it would be if you could know ahead of time that you and your new lover would definitely like each other in the morning. That's what happens when friends become lovers. Later you'll meet Lulu and her good friend

Hank. When Lulu's friend Amanda started to talk about Hank romantically, Lulu knew that she couldn't lose him. She looked at him through new eyes, then told him how she felt. They gave it a try, and suddenly they were on fire!

Rx: Before you go looking for a mate among strangers, check among your friends.

Being best friends and being best lovers are *not* mutually exclusive. In fact, they can make a perfect combination. And here's the best part. Best friends usually share similar points of view—and researchers find that turns out to be the best predictor of long-term bonding. Think about it. All those stimulating debates on dates are going to turn into tedious arguments at home if the issues are family, money, or marriage. His charming banter, his piano-playing skill, and the cut of his suit may count when you bring him to a New Year's Eve party, but they can't predict his capacity for commitment or his sense of responsibility. The extras may count in your fantasy, but it's the basics that count in love. And friends usually have the basics down pat. You've watched his behavior, observed his friendships and family relationships, and, mainly, seen his behavior with you. You know your compatibility extends beyond the dance floor and bedroom. Love is never really blind—only fantasy is!

But don't try to change your friendship with a man into a romance on a lark or just to see if you can. It's worth trying if you really discover that you feel he's perfectly lovable and you think he feels you are too. Then, if it doesn't work out, it was yet one more experience the two of you shared. Remember, though, that trying to change the relationship could feel uncomfortable and hurt the friendship if the "hidden romance" isn't mutual. In other words, be sure the reward is worth the risk, so no matter what the outcome you'll still feel it was worth the try.

10 When to Absolutely Run—Screaming

Okay. We're assuming we're perfectly lovable. We're feeling understanding, patient, and charitable. We're aware of timing and know that it's a numbers game. We're ready to move forward . . . *but not so fast!*

Mixed in with the *maybes*, *possiblys*, and *let's sees* are some absolute NOs. Can you really spot them? Yes. Can you learn when to run, even when the date is fun? Yes. Can you think like a shrink? Yes!

But here's what it takes: knowing the warning signs, actively looking for them, and then paying attention if you find them. Zero tolerance! You can't pretend you didn't notice them. You can't second-guess yourself. You can't give him third and fourth chances just in case you're wrong. No exceptions, no excuses, and no special cases.

There's No Excuse for Abuse

First, run for your life if you find you're dealing with psychological abuse, particularly if you think it's deliberate and not just the result of ignorance or insensitivity. Our psyches cannot tolerate constant criticism, guilt trips, mind reading, bullying, double messages, or even teasing. Our brain goes on constant alert, waiting for an attack, preparing a defense. Our body is always ready for fight or flight, and after a while we become mentally and physically exhausted and our emotional immunity drops. So does our self-esteem. We become susceptible to depression, sleeplessness, irritability, and concentration problems, and then we're feeling helpless or hopeless about the future. Not worth it for love or money!

Next, run even faster if there's any hint of his being physically abusive. One in every three women is assaulted by her partner. Two of every three women battered after marriage had been abused while they were still dating. Forty percent say they knew that their partner had been abusive in the past. In fact, a woman has a higher chance of being injured by her mate than in a car accident, mugging, and rape combined. Don't you be that woman!

Men who have histories of physical abuse usually give very reasonable-sounding explanations: his ex was a witch and pushed him into the abuse, she dared him, she hit first, she humiliated him; he was an alcoholic or a drug user (and now he's not); he was depressed; sex play got out of hand; his family was like that . . . and so on. But here's the bottom line—there's no excuse for abuse. So don't buy his, and don't make up your own for him.

An impulse control problem in the past means the potential for one in the future. The pattern often goes like this: Verbal put-downs lead to condescending and annoyed insults. They lead to threats of physical violence. Threats of violence lead to slaps and shoves. Then come pushing, choking, and even homicide. And this pattern is the same in all socioeconomic groups. So don't let yourself believe that his good education or a wealthy family background makes you safe. Police statistics tells us that a woman is battered every fifteen seconds . . . it's as common as giving birth.

Rx: Always listen to your intuition.

In this case, your self-protective instincts will help you make sure that you're not one of those abuse statistics. *Absolutely run!*

The Green-Eyed Monster

Run just as fast if his jealousy is out of bounds. I know that at first his jealousy might be flattering—it might feel like great love and even give you a sense of power and control, lulling you into thinking he can't live without you. But great jealousy is always a great problem. First, because it often means that he's competing with the entire universe of other men. How exhausting is that? Next, because his jealousy usually means he'll want to isolate you from friends, acquaintances, and even family. Soon your life will be diminished, not enhanced, by the relationship. Then, because a jealous lover is an angry lover, he'll be more likely to want punish than please, even if it was all in his mind. And last but not least, because more than 50 percent of the almost two million women severely battered last year were battered because of sexual jealousy.

If you think you can make him feel secure enough that his jealousy will subside, think again. Extreme jealousy is a real ailment, often a symptom of obsessive-compulsive disorder (OCD) and sometimes of something more serious than that, paranoia. In fact, scientists who study brain neurotransmitters find that those who develop patterns of stalking and passionate jealousy usually suffer from a biochemical imbalance.

I'm sure you've already guessed that you should also be running if it's *your* jealousy that's out of bounds. Especially if you're generally not jealous at all. He's probably making you feel insecure, and whether it's by flirting, flitting, or forgetting dates and details, it's lethal for love.

Insist That He Resist

Run even faster if he is unfaithful to you. In fact, think twice if he is being unfaithful to someone else when he's with you, or if he was unfaithful to his previous partner—even if she forgave him! When this happens in a long-term marriage, there are many things for a wife to consider before bailing out or deciding to stay. But when this happens in a new relationship, why tolerate it or send the message that you would tolerate it? Why bank on the unknown future when you have the well-known past giving you signals loud and clear? You may forgive . . . but you'll never forget.

And don't try to blame anyone but him—especially not the other woman. Surveys and other research tell us that most men *don't* cheat because there's a problem at home. Actually, more than 50 percent of those who cheat say they're happy at home! They tell anonymous polls that they cheated because they wanted variety, because the opportunity just happened, because their best friend was having an affair (which gave them ideas, and someone to cover for them), or because their parents cheated, in that order. But these are all excuses, not an explanations. Besides, even if a guy is truly unhappy at home, don't you want someone who has enough control to wait until he ends one relationship before he starts another one?

So stop blaming yourself if he cheated. It's not you, it's definitely him. The number one reason that faithful men give for *not* cheating isn't greater love, it's greater commitment, it's because "they promised." So if he cheated, it's information about *him*. Take it as information about his character, his capacity for commitment, his modus operandi.

But suppose you're not yet into the heavily committed stage, and he strays. Can you really hold it against him? Yes. Especially if you're heavily into sex with him. He has the rest of his life to see others if it doesn't work out with you. If he can't wait, don't you wait, either—get out of there. Ninety percent of American men say they believe affairs "are always or almost always wrong." Yet one in four do it anyway. Look for one of the other three!

Leave a Liar

Does he lie? We all do—about thirteen times a week. But those are white lies to make others feel good (like "thanks, I love the sweater") or to make ourselves look good ("I'm a sensitive kind of guy"). If he's telling big lies to get himself out of trouble ("the company sent me out of town") or to manipulate ("I'm almost divorced but I have to be home on weekends for the kids"), run!

Habitual liars typically know right from wrong—but they don't particularly care. This makes them smooth and glib, but not invincible. Perhaps more than any other question I'm most often asked: "How do I spot a liar? I keep trusting guys because I know I can be trusted." Here are just a few ways to spot a liar:

- Look for micro expressions: flashes of fear, anxiety, or guilt.

- Note a lack of eye contact.
- Sometimes a higher voice pitch than usual gives them away.
- Spot a false smile: these don't involve the eyes, tend to be lopsided, and can last too long or not long enough.
- Pay attention to excessive blinking. It suggests that he's trying remember lines rather than being spontaneous. Bill Clinton's blink rate famously went up from 35 times a minute to 120 times a minute while being interviewed about Monica Lewinsky.
- Note rapid speech, too. If it sounds like a well-rehearsed lie, it probably is!
- Listen for lots of pauses when he's answering your questions. It can mean he's inventing as he goes along.
- Beware of an overused line he repeats often, word for word.
- Notice if he's always apologizing. We automatically respond to apologies, like "I'm sorry it happened" and "I'm sorry I embarrassed you." In fact, we have to fight *not* to respond to forgive those who apologize . . . and liars know it.

Know the Danger Signals

Believe it or not, the hardest type of liar to spot is the most dangerous type of liar. The sociopathic personality. They know right from wrong but don't care. A sociopath experiences little or no guilt when behaving badly, and little or no pride when doing something good. Sounds as though sociopaths have very little reason to delay gratification or work hard, doesn't it? You're right. Just think how differently you'd live your life if you had little or no conscience! My guess is that you'd look for shortcuts, live for today, and use manipulation to get what you want. That's just what sociopathic guys are like—usually impulsive, sexually promiscuous, and charming, without real connection to anyone. They are treacherous, literally and figuratively. Most sociopaths are not murderers, but most murderers are sociopaths. A chilling thought. Not that you're in mortal danger during a blind date with a sociopath personality. He's more likely to break your heart than your bones. But that's bad enough!

Rx: If a guy seems too good to be true, he probably is.

So think "con man" if he's *everything* you always wanted. And after it becomes obvious that it's an act, don't think you can change him. All the scientific evidence points to the problem being his nature, not his nurture. He is conscience-lite and probably born that way.

So as you listen to him talk about himself, pay attention if you hear that as a *child*:

__ he was expelled or suspended from school for truancy or misbehavior
__ he was arrested for delinquency
__ he ran away from home more than once

__ he shoplifted
__ he vandalized
__ he started fights
__ he drank or used drugs regularly

He may make these behaviors sound funny or fascinating, but they're still warning signs for you. If he doesn't talk about his childhood, see if he has four or more of these *adult* warning signs:

__ he changes jobs a lot—three or four jobs in one year
__ he's unemployed often
__ he often doesn't show up for work
__ he walks off jobs without any prospects for another one
__ he spends money impulsively
__ he doesn't spend much time with his children (if he has any)
__ he doesn't respect the law, and bends or breaks it often
__ he has had many affairs or simultaneous relationships
__ he has had few enduring relationships, few close friends
__ he defaults on debts, child support, alimony, mortgage payments
__ he has excuses for not picking up the check when he's with you
__ he becomes irritable or aggressive if you criticize him
__ he doesn't plan ahead (your dates, his life!)
__ he lies to get out of trouble with you, and with everyone

Only about 3 percent of American men are really sociopaths, but most of them are single since they usually don't have enduring relationships . . . so watch out!

Avoid the [Perpetually] Unemployed

Run if he's fired from his job again and again. It's not about the money, honey! It's about playing well with others, having the capacity to be part of a team, and showing some impulse control. Problems in those three areas are the three most frequent reasons given by bosses for firing an employee. They're also among the top three reasons given by women for filing for divorce.

Could his unemployment be just bad luck? Of course. Could he be unappreciated again and again? Sure. Could he be so smart that his boss was jealous or threatened? Yup. But if he's fired *often*, it's unlikely. Different bosses + same reaction = why give it a try?

Rx: Remember that you're trying to stack the odds in your favor, not beat the odds!

Besides, every time he's fired, he's probably distracted and depressed, and low on libido, self-esteem, and patience, too!

You Don't Need the Needy

Now this may sound strange coming from a therapist, but run if he's a therapy junkie. Lifelong steady customers are usually too self-involved, and they're used to talking about themselves too much. Short-term help when he's in crisis is fine! Twenty years of hand-holding is not. Plus, who wants to compete with a therapist? Need I say more?

Don't Ignore Those Who Came Before

Finally, be ready to run if his children or family will have nothing to do with him—nothing at all. Check out his version of the explanation, of course, but be very cautious, since most ex-wives continue to maintain a relationship with their former husband for the sake of their children. In fact, the nurturing response is so strong in women that they will share custody or at least pretend to cheerfully pass the children to their father every other weekend, despite hurt, anger, and disappointment. You can bet that if she cuts him off completely, there's usually a very serious reason! And you want to know that reason. Let me say it again: the best predictor of future behavior is past behavior. You must have zero tolerance for the red flag man. It's not you, it's him!

Gut Feelings

Did you know that in addition to the brain in our head, we have a brain in our gut? I mean that literally as well as figuratively. There are nerves that travel from the solar plexus to the cerebral cortex and tell the brain about our "gut feelings." These gut feelings, scientists say, serve a basic, vital survival function—they tell us who the good guys are. They tell us whom to like and whom to trust. They tell us when to give it a try. *But they're not always right!* So we'd better look at these gut feelings.

There are basically five male behaviors that reflexively trigger a positive "gut" response from women as early as the first date. Let's take these responses off automatic pilot and return control to our head, instead. Here's the list of behaviors that sounds great but are worth some worry, and the warnings that go with them:

1. Warmth

If he's emotionally open, ready to smile, help, and hug, he's got a point on the likability scale, and studies find we're very likely to give the guy a try.

But here's the warning:

> That rosy glow around him can cloud your vision, so give it time. We are programmed to respond to warmth from the time we're born in order to collect protectors, build a list of backups in case our family fails us, and search for allies among enemies. But we can be fooled. Some guys seem good because they're good at hiding the bad.

There are guys who cheat on women, abuse women, and use women. There are guys who are angry with women, disinterested in women, or afraid of women. There are guys who can't commune or commit. Don't let happy hugs hide the truth. Watch him with his sister, your friends, the neighbor, the waiter, to see if the warmth is for real or just for now.

2. Friendliness

If a guy seems to be a people person, your gut will tell you he's one of the good guys. But watch out, because that friendly style may be only a style—a substitute for real bonding.

The warning goes like this:

> For faux friendly people, one woman typically isn't enough. They need everyone to like them, so they date everyone and become close to everyone (and their family). What seems like special closeness to you may not be special at all to him. It's generic closeness, not genuine closeness.

Jay could turn any night out into a party. Zoe met him at a political fund-raiser, and after one dance she was smiling. He looked right into her eyes when she spoke, knew every word to every rap song, and knew everybody in the room. She felt as though she were with the class president in high school even though she was twenty-six. He took her for a run with his dog the next day, and met her brother that evening and was playing touch football with him by the weekend. He was relaxed and

> natural with her parents, and Zoe felt very lucky. That is, until she ran into Jay with Paulina and her little girl. They were at the movies, and Jay was carrying Paulina's daughter into the theater on his shoulders. Paulina had her arm through his, and her parents were buying the popcorn.

Friendliness was Jay's "thing." He loved being part of a group—any group, all groups. He liked being liked and figured out how to work it. But here's the catch: When Zoe told him that she was hurt by what she saw, Jay looked at her as if she were crazy. "How could you fall for me?" he asked. "What did I do to make you think I could be serious?" Zoe learned that gut feelings are better at warning us about the *no*'s than advising us about the *yes*'s.

3. *Optimism*

If he's upbeat, positive, and encouraging, you probably feel good around him, because attitudes are naturally catching.

But there's a warning here, too:

> When we feel good, we're far less likely to think critically or clearly. In other words, it's not how we feel about what he says that's influencing us—it's how what he says makes us feel! And that's not good enough.

If he sounds like a politician running for office, if his business plans "can't lose" and the trips he's planning are all "awesome," and his promises are nonstop, be careful. You'll suspend your concerns because you want his dreams to come true.

> Martin was a single, never-married Miami real estate broker who was in love with Kristine. He told her that he was planning to leave real estate and open a restaurant in South Beach, and he spent many weekends with her, looking for a great location. The next step, he said, would be to franchise it out. He reassured her that she'd never have to worry about money again, once he was rolling, and that after they had children she could work or stay home as she wished. He asked her where she wanted to build a weekend home, and how she wanted to decorate it. After two years of terrific talk, Martin was still a single, never-married Miami real estate broker, and Kristine moved on.

When you're dealing with a supreme optimist, listen very carefully when he paints fabulous word pictures of a fun-filled future together, and check out his past. If he's really made his own dreams come true, you can begin to trust him with yours. If not, it's time to worry. Keep telling yourself "Let's wait and see" instead of "I can't wait to see!" Tell yourself "Only time will tell" rather than "My time has finally come."

4. *Humor*

If he has a sense of humor, he gets lots of points. Check any of those "What Women Want" surveys and you'll see that we all say we want a guy with a sense of humor. And if he has a sense of humor about *himself*, say most social scientists, he gets even more points—on the trustworthiness scale. We like to be around people who don't take themselves too seriously, because it helps us be less self-conscious ourselves.

The warning?

> A sense of humor and trustworthiness don't necessarily go hand in hand. Just think about politicians and used car salesmen. Sometimes that charming readiness to laugh at himself means he's too thick-skinned or too willing to play the fool just to get what he wants. So, once again, time will tell.

Seth made Gina laugh. He was like Chris Rock, Kevin James, and Ray Romano, all rolled up into one. Most other guys spent their time boasting. Seth made fun of himself instead. She loved that he didn't seem to take himself too seriously. She felt comfortable with him. She didn't try to be perfect because he wasn't perfect, and knew it. Imagine how surprised she was the first time he was openly critical of her in front of their friends. When she told him that she didn't want to be put down in public, he said that since he always put himself down, putting her down was no big deal. He was just kidding around, he said, and she was too sensitive.

Gina tried to be less defensive, but as she became more frequently teased, she traded in Seth's

> sense of humor for the love and loyalty of a humorless accountant.

A sense of humor is seductive. We become charmed and disarmed, literally, and our warning signals can become short-circuited. So make sure the whole package is right for you, or you won't be laughing for long. Once again, the moral of the story is "time will tell."

5. *Sincerity*

Of all the traits on our wish list, most women say the make-or-break, bottom-line, no-compromising-this feature is sincerity. We want men who tell the truth. Sorting through lies, even white lies, is exhausting. And then how do you ever know what you can believe and what you can't?

So here's the warning:

> Judge sincerity by what he does, not what he says! If he tells you he's the kind of guy who likes successful women, wait and see how he handles your phone call telling him you have to work late when you had plans together. If he says he's the kind of guy who's sensitive and caring, see how often he asks you about your day . . . and really listens to your answer!

And make sure he knows *himself* well enough to be truly sincere. He may know how he wants to be seen and what he hopes he means. But until you know if that's who he really is, think to yourself: *He may mean what he says when he says it this week . . . but let's see if he still says it, and means it, next week.*

Rx: Look for a man who's willing to live for you, not "die for you." Living for you is more likely to be required!

Since I'm writing this chapter during a visit to Hollywood, California, let me put it another way. I'll tell you what some say about actors here: "Once they can fake sincerity, they've got it made!" Make sure your new man isn't an actor.

11 When to Worry

There are guys whose behaviors fall between *when to have fun* and *when to run*. They're not quite in the zero tolerance category, but they're not in the clear, either. These are the behaviors that therapists check for when they're working with couples. If they find these behaviors, therapists respond by telling the couple that work is needed because these are old behaviors that interfere with new relationships. How should *you* respond? Don't go on red alert, but your level of concern should go up to orange. They are behaviors that often outweigh the pluses because they are so hard to change without help:

Look for Unfinished Business

Hostile remarks about ex-girlfriends or ex-wives let you know two things.

1. He's still emotionally involved with his past relationships.
2. He hasn't really evaluated *his* role in the failure and is likely to repeat it.

Rx: Ignorance isn't bliss, it's just dumb.

So listen carefully when he's talking nonstop on that first date or after three drinks. The information he'll give you will be priceless, because he'll probably never again be as talkative as at the beginning of the relationship. Don't wait to ask questions until he's so comfortable with you that he's sure there's nothing more to say.

Think Twice About Comparisons

You are different from anyone else he has known, but if he's making constant comparisons that means he's not seeing you as you are and is not yet free to get to know you. He is most likely looking for a "do-over" opportunity—a situation in which he can set up the past again to try to make it come out different this time.

Rx: Find someone who's working on real problems with you, not past problems through you.

We all have baggage, of course. But we don't all take the suitcases everywhere we go. If he still carrying around every sling and arrow, every cut and bruise, every slight and snub, from every date and mate, his arms will be too full to hold you.

If he's willing to try to start new, at least you know he acknowledges his problem, and that makes him just mildly imperfect. If he doesn't realize (or won't admit) that he's doing a do-over, however, that always makes a relationship very difficult and makes him very imperfect. Why? Because he'll overreact to you every time he blends you with many who came before. It will be John against the world of women instead of John and you working it out.

Life is hard enough for two—life is much too hard if he's bringing a gang of ghosts along, too. Suggest a therapist if you both want to give it a try anyway. Don't take on all those phantoms yourself!

Beware of Guerrilla Warfare

If he's plotting and planning revenge, against anyone, about anything, he won't have enough emotional energy to move forward with you.

It may seem like no problem at first. A guy is furious at

his ex but thinks you are perfectly lovable by comparison. He's clear on the differences:

> You're sweet; she's a bitch.
> You're understanding; she's a narcissist.
> You're flexible; she's rigid and demanding.

Great. You thank her for being so bad. But then you think of the past week and realize that he was preoccupied when you were talking over drinks because he's thinking of the fight he had with her that afternoon about custody of their dog. He was preoccupied when you were at dinner because he had just spoken to his lawyer about the latest court battle with her lawyer, and he was preoccupied when he was with your family last weekend because he was thinking of all those years he wasted getting to know and like her family. And with the little time he had left, he was fighting with her on the phone.

Rx: Watch out for angry battles or you'll be hit in the crossfire!

Andrea learned this the hard way.

> Andrea thought Ben was terrific and couldn't imagine how his ex-wife ever let him get away. *She must be crazy*, Andrea thought. Ben said she was.

> He said that everything would be fine at home and then his ex-wife's head would spin as if she were the possessed girl in *The Exorcist* and verbal pea soup would come out of her mouth. For no reason. *Hooray*, thought Andrea. *Lucky for me*.
>
> But Andrea began to find that she had flare-ups of rage at Ben, herself. The first time was when Ben seemed to forget everything he promised during their heart-to-heart talk, even when she reminded him of what they had said. Next, it was when Ben put her down in front of his friends but instead of apologizing told her she had misunderstood him. Then it was when he called a waitress "sweetie," the same nickname he used for her, and insisted that Andrea was creating a problem by getting upset about it.
>
> Just when she was beginning to wonder if his ex (or anyone) could really be that bad, the calls started. At first they were hang-ups, then warnings to stay away from Ben. Andrea felt caught in the middle. On the one hand, she had begun to sympathize with Ben's ex-wife: She felt crazy at times with Ben, too. On the other hand, she was now a focus of his ex-wife's anger.

One solution is to wait before you date anyone dealing with a major life-changing event. No matter how together someone seems to be after a breakup or loss, it takes time before the brain really permanently processes any big change.

Actually, it can take up to two years before we can wake up in the morning and not be startled by recalling a death or divorce or big breakup. So, when in doubt, wait before you date—for your sake.

Pay Attention to His Sad : Glad Ratio

Assess whether he's "down" more than "up." It doesn't matter if it's a biochemical problem, a post-trauma problem, or an attitude problem—it's not *your* problem unless you make it so. Now is when you have the choice, before your lives are entwined. Later may be too late. Life in a relationship is usually hard enough without adding mysterious mood problems, so look for these symptoms of chronic sadness:

- ***Persistent annoyance and criticism***
  Especially if it's loaded with sarcasm or contempt. Even though he may try to disguise this negativity as intellectual impatience, superiority, or machismo, it really means that the guy has no psychological energy for other people—a classical sign of depression. Besides, how much fun can you have with a guy who is like this?

- ***Pessimism***
  Not only about the economy, the political situation, or global warming, but about his personal life, too. If he expects to get fired, worries about his health, and thinks of himself as unlucky, how can you expect him to plan a future with you?

- ***Changes in eating and sleeping patterns***
  Like trouble going to sleep or staying asleep night after night, or eating too much or too little for more than two weeks. These are often the signs that a clinical depression has begun. Encourage him to see a doctor—TLC alone is usually not enough!

Worry About Relationship Amnesia

Beware of the guy who remembers nothing of his past, or pretends not to. "I don't know" is not an encouraging answer to questions like "Why are you still single?" or "Why didn't your marriage work?" If he's never thought about it, you probably don't want to be with him.

If he has thought about it and decided that he was not part of the problem, you probably don't want to be with him. If he's thought about it and knows his role but doesn't want to admit it, you probably don't want to be with him.

But if he wants to figure out what went wrong and is willing to talk about it, asks you for feedback, and accepts it when it comes at him, he's still imperfect (all men are!), but probably a keeper.

When to Give It a Try

So you've decided there's finally a guy with good timing who's ready, willing, and able to get serious. But you're the one who's not sure. *There's got to be a more perfect match*, you're thinking. Then you remember these two basic assumptions:

Always assume that there is a more perfect match for you than the man you're dating, somewhere in the world.

Always assume, however, that if it took you many years to find the imperfect guy you're now dating, it may take you just as many years or more to find a better one.

Maybe he's not so imperfect, you may now be thinking, *at least, not as imperfect as lots of others. Besides, he knows I'm perfectly lovable and that's a plus. How do I know when to stay and when to go?* When to say maybe and when to say no? When is it just shortcomings and when is it "life's too short"?

Start by asking yourself these questions:

Would you really rather be on your own, alone, than wake up next to him every morning, no matter how perfect he thinks you are?

Would you rather watch television and eat Oreos in bed than go to bed with him?

Would you rather grow old reading good books and raising the thermostat than raising children with him?

If the answer is yes to any of these questions, walk away. All the checklists, and case studies, and tips, and primary principles in the world won't make this right.

But make sure you're not trading him in for someone you haven't met yet. No real man can compete with a perfect fantasy—particularly an "imperfect" man. Make sure you're asking yourself if you'd rather *be alone*, *forever*! That's the true test, and insurance against beating yourself up later for letting him get away. If you ask yourself the tough questions and still say, "I'd rather be single," you'll never have to say, "What was I thinking?" You'll know exactly what you were thinking.

Look what happened to Karen:

Tom was the first man Karen dated after a passionate love and devastating breakup. They had pretty good chemistry, she thought, though nothing like the heartrending passion she had shared with her doomed first love. And he was not quite her intellectual equal. But she and Tom were emotionally perfectly suited. He knew just when she'd had a bad day and would draw her a hot bath without asking. He was as fun to talk to about their mutual friends as her best girlfriend. Sometimes she thought he was like her best friend in the second grade who always saved her a seat on the bus. Still, she thought there was probably someone better for her out there, someone she would love the way she'd loved her ex. She often thought about ending it but couldn't quite do it. But she didn't know if she wanted to stay, either. Then one day he proposed and she had to make up her mind. And the thought of saying "no" felt much worse than saying "yes." That was how she decided, and she has never regretted it.

Less Imperfect Than You Think

So how about the "keepers," the good guys, and the "diamonds in the rough"? You think you've found one, but you need some reassurance. After all, he's not perfect. You've been told to watch, worry, and wait by everyone in your life, including me, and now you want to know when *not* to worry. So, here's a checklist of demerits and extra credits—compiled from many years of working with couples:

- ***If a guy is perfectly lovable but has some small, annoying habits he picked up in the past (like grunting softly when he eats or talking and making noise in the movies), give him a Not-Very-Imperfect rating and try before you say bye.***
  Annoying habits tend to fade into the background when you get used to him (desensitization), become endearing if he accepts yours (mutual admiration), or can be changed once he's aware of them (behavior modification). If he's not interested in changing them, lower his rating. If he is interested in changing them, change one of yours as part of the deal.

- ***If a guy is willing just to listen sometimes when you're talking about your own problems, without telling you how to "fix" your problem, rate him Worth-a-Try and forget good-bye for now.***
  "Just" listening is difficult for a guy, and it takes real effort and caring. It feels passive, guys say, and passivity is usually not their style, so it may not come with his package. You may have to add it. Try telling him many times that just saying things out loud helps you. Try telling him that he's a great listener. Try telling him that just hearing your own words out loud gives you more perspective than thinking the same things silently,

alone, in the middle of the night. Try telling him how much you appreciate his lending you his ear and shoulder—without the advice that usually goes with it. If he gets it, he's a keeper!

- ***If a guy is willing to talk about the relationship, this is a good sign.***
  And if you want him to continue to talk about things that bother you, make sure you don't start the discussion by pointing a finger or start sentences with the word "You." To encourage him to keep talking, start with "I" (as in, "I'm a bit sensitive when it comes to . . .") and share responsibility for the problem (as in, "We're not so good at . . .").

Rx: Talk with him, not at him.

- ***If a guy helps out around the house, rate him Unusual.***
  He gets extra credit, because statistics say most guys don't—or, at least, they don't help out enough. In fact, divorce lawyers say the number one pet peeve of busy working women is that their mate doesn't do his share of the housework. Even men who are supportive of their mate's career aren't more likely to help out than guys who aren't. So drop some papers instead of straightening up when he comes over and see what he does. If he bends down to pick them up, he gets to go to Round Two.

- ***If he's able to tolerate your anger once in a while, appreciate it.***

  When men feel criticized, they usually become defensive. Then comes the rebellion reflex. Next, "She's never happy with me. She's probably going to dump me," and finally, "The hell with her." In other words, he typically responds to your anger with more anger, and by the time the sequence passes, you could be going out the door. So if your guy can tolerate your anger without getting defensive, it's a huge plus. If he can't, don't sweat it, either. This a typical dance, and the rhythm is easily changed . . . by you. Here's how.

  Make the issue about *you*. Say "I get upset when . . ." He'll be able to listen to what you're saying, and if he really cares he'll make some changes to please you. If he doesn't seem to care that you are bothered, strike one. If he uses your "sensitivity" against you, strike two. If he calls it "your problem" the next time it comes up, strike three!

  Also, make sure you're honest: Are you really hurt, not angry? If you're constantly hiding your vulnerability from him (and from yourself as well) by acting angry rather than insulted or confused, you'll both begin to think he's making you miserable.

  And, last but not least, make sure you're clear about your goals before you tell him what's bothering you about the relationship. If the problem is your excuse for bailing out, don't say it's something you want to work on. If the problem is something that's not too important to you, save your bargaining chips. If the problem is something that's make-or-break, attack the problem, but not him. If you attack him, you may prove that he was wrong and win the battle, but you're really likely to lose him. And always, if you've got a complaint, don't bring it up until you've thought of a few ways of making it better.

Rx: Communicate to be heard, not to win.

- ***If a guy makes you smile a lot, rate him Imperfect, but Very-Lovable even if he has other problems.***
Give him a second look not only because this says something about him, but because it also says something about you. You must have good feelings for him, because if you were angry, annoyed, or disappointed, you wouldn't be laughing.

- ***If a guy is a good friend as well as a lover, give him the highest ratings of all.***
Did you know that the latest studies of successful relationships found that the main ingredient is feeling that you're spending your life with someone who is on your side, who sees you as a teammate, who is your best friend? Karen never read the studies, but her gut told her that her "best friend who would always save her a seat on the school bus" was a keeper.

It may be much too soon to know if he'll be a good friend to you, but it's never too soon to find out if he's been a good friend to others. I can't say this often enough or loud enough.

Rx: The best predictor of future behavior is past behavior.

If he has friends from high school, college, the old neighborhood, old jobs, summer camp, even a few old girlfriends, don't feel competitive. If he has time for them, he'll have time for you. If he's loyal to them, he'll be loyal to you. If he cares about them, he'll care about you. Not because they (and you) are all so very special, but because that's what he's like—it's obviously his nature. And a nature like that is worth nurturing.

13 Why You Must Fall Wildly in Love!

You've learned to have zero tolerance for the man who doesn't find you perfectly lovable, and you've vowed to meet halfway the man who does. But don't think that male imperfection means that you have to settle. Settle for no less than falling wildly in love.

> Lulu didn't start out loving Hank. In fact, she pined for her heartless ex, Peter. Hank was just a friend who would stay up with her all night on the phone while she blamed herself for her shortcomings un-

> til she fell asleep from crying. But then one day, Lulu's friend Amanda started to eye Hank romantically, and right then Lulu knew that she couldn't lose him. She told him how she felt, they decided to give it a whirl as a couple, and they were suddenly on fire!

Here's the lesson. You can go from being "just friends" to falling wildly in love just by changing how you look at someone. Lulu started looking at Hank through Amanda's eyes, and the new perspective gave her new information about him—and about herself. They went from zero to sixty and things got pretty sexy pretty quickly.

So what changed? Hank says he was in love with Lulu all along. But Lulu was so busy beating herself up for not being everything Peter wanted that she didn't realize that Hank was everything *she* wanted. In other words, she was so busy looking at herself that she didn't even see Hank. If she had assumed she was perfectly lovable, she would have concluded that Peter had the problem, not her. If she had assumed she was perfectly lovable, she would have seen that Peter wasn't and Hank was!

Now Lulu and Hank are long married and say it's the best friend part of their relationship that gets them through daily life, but my point is that everyone deserves to feel crazy in love at first. And every time Lulu looks at Hank through other women's eyes—and she makes sure she does it often—the passion is there again. She learned that once we find someone who is lovable, we can fall wildly "in love" with him. It's not something that just happens. It's something we can help happen.

Love at First Sight?

In a perfect world, a perfect woman would meet a perfect man and it would be love at first sight. In the real world, perfectly lovable women meet imperfect men and keep waiting to feel love at first sight. Is there really such a thing? And does it lead to everlasting happiness? The answer is yes and no. *Yes*, there can be a happy outcome for those who fall in love at first sight; but *no*, it isn't likely and it isn't often love. The characteristics of that kind of "crush" and love are not only different but diametrically opposed:

- A crush can be one-sided, but *a real love relationship always involves two*.
- A crush makes us feel self-conscious; *love helps us feel self-confident*.
- A crush can be based on external characteristics; *love is based on inner character*.
- A crush can occur when opposites attract, but *love is based on our similarities*.
- A crush interferes with our concentration at school, work, or home; *love helps us toward higher achievement*.
- A crush helps us escape from daily life for a while; *love helps us manage daily life more easily*.
- A crush helps us pretend we could be different by being

with someone who is different; *love helps us "get real" and be ourselves*.

Quite a difference!

Rx: Enjoy your crushes, but don't confuse them with love.

Don't confuse being upset and being in love, either. *Of course not*, you're thinking. But we do it all the time.

Let's face it—even in these liberated times, men are still more likely to make the dates and take the initiative. They are still more likely to be the ones to propose everything, from a particular restaurant to a living arrangement to marriage. So we women spend more time waiting—waiting to get telephone calls, waiting to find out if there will be a future. The longer we wait, the more we fear disinterest or desertion. The more fear we feel, the more visceral reactions we have: pounding heart, shaking hands, knotted-up stomach. The more visceral reactions we notice, the more we conclude that we are in love! We say to ourselves, *If he can make me feel this upset, I must really care about him*.

Wrong. Sometimes we're agitated because we're angry at rudeness, anxious about being alone, insecure about our popularity, or feeling a loss of a sense of control. Those reactions do not automatically mean that we're wildly in love. Although psychologists and grandmothers agree that keeping the other person guessing does seem to increase that person's feelings of infatuation, it's an illusion that doesn't last very long.

Rx: Don't confuse aggravation and infatuation.

Love should make you feel good—if you feel bad, it's not love. Wait for the real thing.

The Real Thing

How do you know if your love is real? Listen to the songs, poems, stories, and love letters written by others in love. Your experience may feel unique, but the love experience is really so universal that descriptions of "eros" by the ancient Greeks will sound like descriptions of "luv" by the latest rapper. Here's what you'll hear:

> Love makes you feel strong, generous, and confident—and devoted to the man who brings out those feelings.
> Love makes you feel connected to him—body to body, mind to mind, and soul to soul.
> Love makes you feel beautiful—inside and out.
> Love makes you feel loving.

The love experience is so recognizable because the capacity for love is inborn; it's *ours*. It's part of our human nature. We can choose to give it, or not. We can let it grow, or not. It's ours. If one romance doesn't work, we can give our love again. It's ours. If you've never felt real love, let me assure you that you will know it when you feel it.

And even though I'm saying that we should settle for no less than falling wildly in love, I'm not suggesting that we are, or should be, hopeless romantics. Just the opposite. Sure, we read more romantic novels than men, see more "chick flicks," and read more articles on "How to Pump Up the Love," but our interest in romance is usually *recreational.* In our daily lives, we women are breathtakingly practical.

Not only are we *not* infatuated more easily or more often than men, but the reverse is true. When Dr. Zick Rubin asked a thousand college students, "If a man or woman had all the qualities you desired, would you marry this person if you were not in love with her or him?" he found that 65 percent of the male students said they wouldn't marry if they weren't "in love," but 76 percent of the females said they would marry the person. I think they meant that they didn't have to be "in love" with a guy to marry him—they just had to find him lovable.

Nonetheless, women are not wrong in believing that their infatuations are more intense than those of men. But—and this is important—only to a point. The cycle of mind-body-mind infatuation does not go on forever. Eventually the body's emergency system and the mind's passion become exhausted. Like all peak emotions, infatuation passes. It may end by fading slowly into memories, or changing loudly into rage or quietly into despair. It may even grow steadily into love. Whatever the eventual outcome, *infatuation is al-*

ways and only a stage of feeling, not a final state. Sometimes sadly, sometimes happily, we recognize that this is so . . . but not until it's over.

Having It All

> Gina's mother always told her, "Find a nice guy who can also make money." "What about falling in love?" Gina asked. "Find a nice guy who belongs to the church, votes Republican, wants a family, will come here for holidays, and can support you," her mother answered. "But Mom," said Gina, "what about falling in love?" "Find a nice guy instead," said her mother again, "because if you want to fall in love, too, you're asking too much and you'll be waiting forever!" "Then I'll wait," said Gina. "I want both."

Actually, Gina's mother was wrong. Gina can have both. Studies show that, at best, finding a man who is similar in age, education, and political leanings narrows the field of suitable candidates down by about 50 percent. But that still leaves more than half the eligible population as possibilities, since most of us surround ourselves with people who are broadly similar to us anyway. Many of those eligible men are sure to find Gina perfectly lovable. All Gina has to do is find one who she feels is lovable, too.

And that's all *you* have to do. Find one lovable person

who finds you lovable in return. It's a numbers game. It's about timing. It's about self-respect and zero tolerance for anyone who doesn't treat you with respect. It's about knowing when it's not you, and then what to do. It's about recognizing when to have fun and when to run, when to meet him halfway and when to say "no way." It's about no self-blame and no man-made pain.

Oh yes, one more thing if you want to have it all. After you've found Mr. Imperfect but Perfectly Lovable, love him. Love him because loving feels so good, and it's so good for you. It's a natural human capacity, and the more you use it, the more it will grow. If it isn't appreciated and reciprocated, find someone who will love your love. And while you're looking, don't deprive yourself of the joy of loving. Make a list of your loved ones, and make sure that you're on that list, too.

14 How Do You Know He's the One?

If you've spent years, as some of us do, equating love with longing, measuring love by how miserable a man makes you, it can be surprisingly tough to date the *It's Not You* way. Once you've stopped blaming yourself for every date that didn't work, after you've stopped trying to change yourself for anyone else but yourself, after you've found a guy who finds you perfectly lovable as you are, after you've decided that he's perfectly lovable, too, and decided to give it a try, how do you know if you really love him or are just happy to be loved?

For some it seems to be easy. They tell you, "I just knew

he was the one." Maybe it happened to one or more of your friends. Maybe you saw it in a movie or TV show or read about it in a book. It usually means they had that gut feeling we talked about in Chapter 12, one "IT" moment in which they realized that the person across the table was the one they wanted forever.

> My friend Colleen swears by the long car trip rule. She knew her fiancé, Zach, was the one after driving from New York City to Washington, D.C., together. For one thing, they never fought over control of the radio. They took turns and most of the time picked what the other would have chosen anyway. But two other things happened on that ride, too. One had to do with silence and the other with sound. At one point, while they were creeping along the New Jersey Turnpike in bumper-to-bumper traffic, they both began belting out Bruce Springsteen's *Born to Run* when it came on the radio. Once they realized they didn't feel silly singing out loud, they sang along to many tunes during the long ride. But there were quieter times, when neither said or sang anything at all. "That we both felt so comfortable in our own thoughts that we didn't feel like we had to be constantly making conversation made me realize that this guy was one I'd been searching for my whole life. I could picture us making trips like this with our children and grandchildren," she said.

When an "IT" moment like this does happen, it usually means the brain in your head and the brain in your gut are teaming up to tell you to go for it. And if that feeling comes after enough time with someone who finds you lovable, you probably should.

That moment happened to Angie when she was sick with a stomach flu and her boyfriend, Joe, spent the weekend by her side, taking care of her. They had only dated for a few months and it was the first time he had ever seen her looking less than perfectly put together and acting anything but totally in control of the situation. By the end of that weekend, both Joe and Angie had seen different sides of each other and loved each other more because of them.

But gut feelings are few and far between, and sometimes misinformed. So here are some additional ways to figure out if he's working his way into your heart—if he is indeed the one for you.

The Soul Mate Test

Ask ten married couples what made them realize they were meant for each other and you'll probably get ten very different answers. You may even get different answers from each spouse! But the theme is usually the same: Something made each one feel the other was a soul mate. What does that mean? That means that each found that the other shared a core value or priority or goal or belief—one that was so deep in their hearts that it was part of how they defined themselves.

> For Morgan, it was children that make her think her boyfriend, Gary, was the one for her. They had spent a romantic weekend at the beach. While cuddling in bed, they started talking about wanting to raise children with old-fashioned values. Even though they'd never discussed marriage before, they both realized it was something they wanted, and before you knew it, they were naming the children they would have someday. "I saw a side of Gary had never seen before and I knew he was serious about this. It wasn't just lighthearted pillow talk. I knew he wanted children as much as I did, and the fact that we so easily agreed on names blew me away," she said.

If you think you may be in love with a soul mate but you're not sure, ask yourself if you and your man live in the same psychological world. Do you share similar attitudes about family, friends, God, pets, weekend activities, money, board games, food, music, sex, movies—some of the above, all of the above? You don't have to be carbon copies of each other to feel like soul mates, but every overlap will make you feel like less of a stranger in a strange land and more of a woman who's found her emotional home. My friend Connie calls it the "armpit" test. When you're sitting together with his arm around you and your head on his shoulder, just listening to him talk, does what he says make you want to stay right there in his armpit? If the answer is yes, you've probably found a soul mate, and your love for him will likely grow.

The Smile Test

You may remember that I've warned you not to confuse aggravation with infatuation. "If he can get me that upset, I must really care," you may have said to yourself in the past. But not anymore. The only thing getting upset *really* means is that he's upsetting. If you want to find out how much you care about him, ask yourself how often he makes you smile. I don't mean by entertaining you, by telling jokes or acting like a clown. I mean by being himself. If being with him makes you smile with pleasure, if hearing from him makes you smile with pleasure, if thinking about him makes you smile with pleasure, you must really care. And there's a very good chance you care enough to call it love. Give him a point on the love scale.

> Patti knew she loved being with Mark. He had a wild sense of humor that always kept her in stitches. But there were other things she loved about him too—the gentle way he treated his aging mother; the horsey rides he gave her three-year-old niece, even when he was exhausted from a long day at work; the calls he would make to her before she fell asleep at night so he'd be the last person she spoke to at the end of the day. But she didn't realize how much in love she really was until her friends began teasing her about her "glow." "They told me it must be love because I had a perma-grin on my face every time they saw me. And if Mark called me on my cell phone while I

> was with them, I'd immediately break out in a huge smile that would last the rest of the night. Even my parents noticed it and said they didn't ever remember me being so happy with another man."

Mark must have had the same "perma-grin," too, because they got married and are happily awaiting the birth of their first child. Even if your relationship with a guy who makes you smile all day long doesn't lead to marriage, it's a good barometer for the future.

The Pleasing Test

It sounds like a cliché, but loving someone usually means wanting that someone to be happy. In fact, making him happy becomes as natural and automatic as making yourself happy. We learn what he likes and wants and recite the list to anyone who will listen:

> "We went for seafood last night because Frank loves shellfish."
>
> "I'm a Red Sox fan because Travis lives for them."
>
> "Matt loves the beach so I'm taking him to the Hamptons for his birthday."

If you find that his preferences are getting noticed by you, and getting equal time, you're probably in love. This is not to say that you lose yourself, sacrifice yourself, or put yourself second. This is to say that you find opportunities to make him happy because he makes you happy. It becomes a delight, not a chore. You feel generous, not resentful. He takes pleasure in your happiness and you return the compliment. You want to please him, but not in a 1950s sitcom wife kind of way. Pleasing him and making him happy just come easily to you now.

> That's what happened to Alison when she became involved with Thomas. She knew she was in deep when she walked blocks out of her way to stop at his favorite deli to get his favorite pasta salad—and didn't mind it. The look on his face when she served it was worth it, she told herself. When her sister, Anna, came to visit and saw all the little things Alison did to please Thomas, she couldn't stop teasing her. "You're worse than Mom. Remember how we used to make fun of the way she doted on Daddy, making sure he had his tea brewed just right every night after dinner?" Anna said. Alison laughed and then told her there was a big difference. "Mom waited on Daddy hand and foot and he never thanked her, never really appreciated her," she said. "Thomas always thanks me—and he also gives back. Literally. When I'm tense or had a bad day at work, he gives me great back rubs. He also brings flowers home because I love them and drinks white wine with me when I know he'd really rather have beer!"

A guy like Thomas, who respects and appreciates all you do for him—and does his best to make you happy, too, is definitely a keeper.

The Scan Test

As much as it's human nature to bond and pair off, it's also human nature, say ethologists, to scan for additional or future partners. And let's face it, there are cute guys all over, and you've probably had years of scanning practice. If you find that you've stopped scanning, it's a great sign that your guy might be the one.

> Danielle knew Rob was "the one" when she and her friends were at a dance club for a girls' night out and she just couldn't stop thinking about him. It was the first time she realized how much she missed him when they were apart. What she didn't realize was that she had stopped "looking." But her friends noticed it. Her friends were checking out the men, asking her opinion on who had the best butt, biggest biceps, or killer smile, and she just couldn't get into it. "Uh-oh," they teased. "Danielle is a goner. You started the rating system we use for guys and now you don't even want to look." *Yup,* she thought, *I'm a goner.* And for the first time in her life, as much as she enjoyed hanging out with the girls, she felt uncomfortable with their flirting.

Love first narrows our emotional focus to one person, then moves us toward that person, and finally keeps us with that person. For Danielle, the journey seems to have begun. As the lyrics say: "I only have eyes for you . . ."

The Time Test

If you love someone, you don't need studies to tell you that you want quantity, not just quality, when it comes to spending time together. It's not dependency or insecurity I'm talking about—it's the pleasure of his company. If you find that you're asking him to help you buy tires for your car, and giving up mall time alone to have movie time with him, give him one more point on the love scale.

> Tasha had always been very independent. When she dated a man, she set the times and places they would meet, and she never allowed one guy to take up too much of her time. Every week she made sure to keep time for Tasha, whether it be shopping, a trip to the spa, or spending time with her best friends. Her pals knew Tasha was seriously in love when she began cutting back her girls' nights out after she starting dating Ty. Tasha, who had never been much of a sports fan, would meet Ty several nights a week during baseball season to watch his favorite team. She invited him to her grandmother's for the family's Sunday dinners. And as much as

> she loved getting dressed up to go out to nice restaurants, she began ordering a pizza or Chinese food to be delivered when Ty came over—and said it was just as much fun. She still felt independent. But now she felt lucky in love, too.

If you don't want him to leave at the end of the date or hope he calls you before you fall asleep, it's likely you're finding him lovable. If time spent away from him seems like "in between" time, marking time, waiting time, or even meaningless time, it's likely that you're falling in love. If he seems to want more time together, too, it's likely you're both in love. If the feeling grows, it's usually the real thing.

The Package Deal Test

Does he tell juvenile jokes? Does he dance without rhythm or insist on getting his hair cut much too short? And do you think of all those quirks as just part of the package? If you do, you do love him in some way. You know no guy is perfect, but some guys' imperfections rub you the wrong way. His don't. They're just there. You cluck your tongue at him and roll your eyes, but you're still there, too.

> Robin hated preppy guys, probably because she grew up in an affluent area that was teeming with them. She even chose an urban college so she'd be away from the frat boy scene and hopefully meet more diverse men. And she did, dating men who

> were very different from the preps and jocks that populated her hometown. Then she went home for the holidays and met Brad. He was a cousin of one of her high school friends. There he was in all his preppy glory—Polo shirt, khakis, and Topsiders, with no socks of course. And she couldn't take her eyes off him. They talked for hours the night they met and exchanged phone numbers and e-mail addresses so they could keep in touch. As she got to know him better, Robin discovered Brad had lots of quirks even beyond the preppy outfits that normally drove her crazy. He was a slow driver and hated to e-mail. He'd wear the same ratty pair of sweats for days on end. He'd forget to give her messages if he picked up the phone when she was in the shower. He loved horror movies and she couldn't stand them. Brad seemed like the last man on earth that Robin would hook up with, and yet she couldn't seem to get very upset with any of his idiosyncrasies. What used to be downright annoying with other guys, she actually found endearing with Brad. When she found herself heating up the microwave popcorn so they could watch all the *Alien* movies together, Robin knew this was love.

And that's the way it happens sometimes. You don't even realize it, but suddenly there's this man with all his crazy qualities, and you can either explain them away or realize that they just don't matter because they're part of what makes him so special to you.

The "True You" Test

Here's the best test of all. Do you feel that you can show him all of you and that he'll think of *your* idiosyncrasies as just part of the package? If you are that natural around him, you must trust him to know that you're perfectly lovable and love him enough to test him. Don't make the mistake of thinking that becoming comfortable means that you are "just friends" or that attraction and passion are at an end. Real love stands the test of time and the "true you" test, because it makes us want to stay together long enough not only to have children, but to raise them, too—and enjoy each other after they've grown.

> Karina knew that one of her worst traits was her quick temper, and she usually tried hard to keep it in check at work and around new people. Those who knew her best knew it could flare up and that she usually just needed to blow off some steam to get back to the task at hand. She had been dating Greg for about six months before he got a glimpse of her famous temper. Karina thought for sure that was the last she would see of him. But he called the next day: "Is the coast clear," he joked, "or is it still stormy seas?" They both laughed and she felt better about the situation. When they met up later that day, Karina started to apologize, but he stopped her, telling her that he admired her for not putting up with other people's nonsense and for letting them know it. She was afraid that he would push

> her away, but instead he embraced her, and she knew that he was someone she needed to keep in her life for as long as he'd let her.

When you don't worry about what you look like in the morning or on a long weekend, you know you're beginning to feel comfortable with your man. When you let your hair down, literally and figuratively, with him, you're definitely in the zone with him. When he stays, he is in the zone too.

The Light-Up Test

Do you light up when he comes into the room? After a hard day's work, do you come to life when he rings your bell? Do you go back to work with double energy after a phone conversation with him? If so, researchers will tell you that you're probably in love. They find that certain parts of our brain's "reward center" are stimulated just by looking at someone we love, and that center then increases its output of neurochemicals that increase concentration, energy, and elation.

> A corporate lawyer who worked crazy hours, Kerry used to just crawl home and curl up on the couch after a long day at the office. She didn't want to talk to anyone and would let the phone calls go to voice mail. Dinner was usually takeout, a solitary salad, or a frozen Lean Cuisine, then she'd fall into bed—alone. Then she met Sam and found that she

> couldn't wait to see him at the end of her day. Her feelings for him were giving her adrenaline she never knew she could muster. He'd pop into her mind at the oddest times during the day, and just the thought that she'd see him later would give her a burst of energy to whiz through the paperwork piled up on her desk. They never went more than two days without seeing each other after work. On the weekends, they'd spend hours together just hanging out and were never too tired to make love.

Now, of course, this infatuation stage usually passes before the exhaustion does us in, but if it's love the "lighting up" part lasts and lasts. Even years later, partners still get a silly smile when they look at a picture of their loved one or something else that reminds them of special times spent with that person. I have a letter from a married man about ninety years old who says that he's watching his wife walk up the driveway as he writes and still feels himself fill with delight and joy when he sees her. This is the kind of love to look for. This is the kind of love I hope we all find!

Being Loved vs. Being in Love

Let's suppose that you're still not clear about this love thing. Let's suppose that the guy you're with is a perfectly nice man and that he treats you wonderfully. Let's suppose that you feel happy when you're with him. You feel special because he clearly adores you, bringing you presents and going out of his way to take you places he knows you'll like. Let's suppose that you tell yourself you love him but something is holding you back from making it a committed relationship. Chances are that you aren't in love with him, at least not the way he's in love with you. You are taking pleasure in being loved by him, but you're probably not giving him back that same pleasure. Don't make yourself feel bad. Remember the first assumption: You're perfectly lovable . . . not picky, pushy, or a princess. If he is not the one that you know deep in your heart is your perfect match, then you should end it because it's not fair to him, even though part of you loves him.

On some level you know this already. In my national survey I found that women are far more likely to end a relationship than men are. Ninety percent of men reported being jilted, whereas only 61 percent of women said they had been dropped.

And chances are that it won't work anyway, even if you decide to stay with him longer. Why? Because sooner or later, your partner will know the truth, and that could be devastating to him and to the relationship. Jay Segal, Ph.D., of Temple University, surveyed more than two thousand college students and found that 90 percent of them had been jilted at some time because they were more "in love" than the other person. The more involved person is usually so needy, possessive, or sensitive that his or her partner feels guilt and resentment. On the other hand, among couples that rate themselves equally in love and involved, social psychologist Zick Rubin, Ph.D., found that only 24 percent broke up.

So keep looking for that guy who finds you perfectly lovable, and make sure that you find him perfectly lovable, too. Now, fall wildly in love!

15 How Do You Know If He's for Real?

Perfectly lovable women don't waste time with men who don't treat them that way. But how do you know what a guy really feels? It's no secret that men can say that they love you, and even mean it when they say it, really mean it, but then never get around to committing to you. We all know women who've spent way too much time with men who say all the right things—and do none of them. Many of us have *been* those women. So once you've found a guy who may be perfectly lovable to you, how do you know if he's for real? There are clear clues. Look for them and practice zero tolerance for guys who are clue-less.

First, forget the fairy tales. If his dialogue sounds like a romance novel and his moves seem perfect, beware. It usually doesn't mean he's in love; it usually means he's well rehearsed! I'm not trying to burst your bubble, but as Grandma used to say, if it's seems way too good to be true, it probably is. A guy who goes over the top with love notes, soul-searching talk, and constant comments about how amazing you are just might be sweet-talking you. Real feelings can be a bit daunting and often make men feel somewhat overwhelmed. They are more likely to be looking for a sign from you before they risk putting their heart out there where it can get broken. In other words, if it comes too easy, it *is* too easy. He should be having a harder time of it. Sure, not everyone is that way, but there certainly are plenty of men who compensate for too little feelings with too many romantic words and textbook actions. So if he shows up for the first date with one red rose, remember: that rose wasn't a gift for *you*, it was decoration for *him*.

On the flip side, one clear clue that he really *is* into you is some nervousness. As I said, when most men are falling for you, they are just as anxious as you are and hold back a bit. They don't go around telling you how they feel at first, partly because they don't want to get hurt or turn you off, and partly because they think, *This is for real. I don't want to screw it up*. So look past what he says or doesn't say and take a look at his daily actions—they speak louder than words.

If he wants you in his life, he'll make you part of his life. It's a clear clue that he's for real if he's introducing you to his friends, his coworkers, and his family. A man in love includes you in his plans and is excited for you to meet all the people in his life. He doesn't make excuses or keep you in a separate box. Instead he wants you to become part of his life and he makes an effort to make it happen. If he's into you, he doesn't act one way around you (warm) and another when he's with you around his friends (cool). Sure, he may act a little more like a guy's guy around them, but he won't be a totally different person. If he's for real, he'll act real. You will pretty much know the same guy that his friends and family seem to know.

The other clear clue that he finds you perfectly lovable? He wants to be part of *your* life, too. He cares about meeting your family and friends. He takes time to talk to them and get to know them when he meets them. He cares about them liking him, not for his ego but because he wants them to pass on the good word. He wants to be part of your life so he tries doing things you like. Maybe he's never been much of a morning person, but he makes an effort to get up with you on the weekends. Or he has no clue about art but will spend time with you at the museum. He's not your clone (you don't want that, either), but he's willing to try and he's interested.

Back to Basics

Some clues are so obvious that you'd think we don't even have to talk about them, but we do, because we forget to look for them when we're in love ourselves. Instead of stepping back and judging his actions, we just assume that he feels the same way we do no matter what he says and does, or we try so hard to please that we jump too fast and too high. So back to basics. Here are the questions to ask yourself:

Does he make long-range plans?

Last-minute calls and dates are fine as extras, but not as the basics. Any guy who gives you a line about wanting to keep things spontaneous is doing just that—giving you a line.

> When Nancy was dating Ron, they had a lot of fun when they were together, but actually *getting* together was a problem. Every night of the week he had something else going on, whether it was dinner with a client or his standing Wednesday night poker game. He ran his own company, did volunteer work, and was on a local hockey team. The only times they saw each other was when he'd call her at the last minute, say five P.M., to get together for dinner or a movie that night. When they were together he never ended the date talking about the next time they'd see each other. She told herself and her friends that she admired him for being so active and starting his own company. "He's got a lot going on," she'd say. It went on like this for months until he finally called her and said he was engaged (oh, *that's* what he was so busy with!).

Yes, that's a drastic case, but if a guy is into you, he'll make time for you, whether he's a CEO or a senator. He'll bring you on the business trip or meet you for lunch or invite you to the hockey game. If he's *that* busy, he'll actually want to make plans in advance so that he doesn't miss having you on his calendar and as part of his hectic life.

Rx: Guys who are really in love, really love to make plans.

Men in love are thinking ahead and worrying about someone else tying up your time first. If you don't believe me, ask any guy you know who's ever been in love (your brother, an uncle, your father). I hear what they say in my office and read what they say when surveyed. Guys tend to fall harder and hang on longer. The chase makes them nervous but also keeps them interested.

> Tod was a last-minute type of guy. He didn't plan his weekends, his holidays, or his life. He loved to wake up each day without any commitments (except work) hovering over his head, as he would say. Then one Saturday night he met Kris in the Hamptons and heard himself asking her if she was going to be around the following Saturday night, too. She said she would and gave him her phone number. He wondered how many other guys had asked her out, too, since he saw at least five others trying to hit on her. By Tuesday he had called to confirm. By Friday he was looking forward to seeing her. In fact, he was so focused on getting to-

gether with her and so worried that she would cancel that their plans never felt like a confining commitment. He called and planned for weeks after that. Until he didn't. The one time Tod left the weekend open-ended and called on Saturday morning from the road on his way out to the Hamptons, Kris sounded delighted to hear from him but said she had already made other plans—sorry. Tod realized that seeing Kris was something he was *choosing* to do and made sure that he reserved weekends from then on.

Rx: Have zero tolerance for the man who won't make plans.

Does he plan time alone with you?

Going out with the gang is fun up to a point, but you can't be a couple if you're never a twosome. If he finds you perfectly lovable, he'll look forward to being alone with you. If a guy quickly enfolds you into his social life—takes you home, to meet his friends, to office parties, and to look for a car—he might just be a social animal. Find out if his friends and family have met *all* the women he's dated. If they have, assume that you're not The One but just one of many.

If he's happy just looking at you, that's a good sign.
If he suggests getting away together, that's a good sign.

If he develops a routine for just the two of you (for example, he gets the bagels on Sunday morning, you cook the eggs), that's a good sign.

In other words, if he doesn't seem to want lots of time alone with you (and not just time in bed), don't bother. It's not you, it's him!

Never-ending group dates are for teenagers, and if he can't be alone with you, he's probably still an emotional teenager. It's not you, it's him.

Anyone who can't spend time one on one can't be part of a couple. You don't want him. It's not you, it's him.

Does he remember the big things—and some little things, too?

He should. It's the work of Mother Nature! When we fall in love our brain chemistry actually changes in some ways and our memory for things associated with our beloved is heightened, so remembering where we went to school and what kind of ice cream is our favorite should come naturally to a guy in love. He may not remember *everything*, of course, but if he remembers *nothing*, zero tolerance! He's not in love and he should be gone. Choose among the guys who pick up where you left off the last time you were together, not those who start from the beginning each time you talk.

Rx: Wait for someone who listens to what you say rather than just waiting for his turn to talk.

Does he try to impress you?

If he's falling for you, he'll want you to fall for him, too, and he'll automatically try to impress you. But that doesn't mean telling you about his high-powered career, bragging about his plasma TV, or showing you his fancy cars. That's not love—that's narcissism. A guy who finds you perfectly lovable will try to impress you by putting the spotlight on *you* instead. He'll try to make a good impression on your best friend, take you to a restaurant you casually mentioned you'd like to go to, and really listen when you talk. He sees your relationship as the best thing that ever happened to him and wants everyone to know it. He'll do whatever he can to win you over. It's love.

Does he get jealous?

Not obsessively so, of course. We're not talking about infatuation turned pathological. Jealousy that leads to unfounded suspicion is not a sign of love; it's a sign of possessiveness and can lead to stalking and even violence. So when you see this kind of jealousy, as I said before, run! Don't flatter yourself, don't pass go—just run!

I'm talking about the kind of jealousy that lets you know he believes every man in the room wishes he were with you, the kind that makes him see you as the essence of attractiveness and makes him assume everyone else thinks so, too. I'm talking about the kind of jealousy that makes him ask if you care for him and makes him reassure you that he cares for you. I'm talking about the kind of jealousy that leads him to call to say good night when he's on a business trip to make sure you're home and to let you know that he's in for the night, too. If he seems into you but he's okay with you dating others, doesn't mind if you flirt with another man when you're with him, and thinks it's fine if you're not sexually exclusive, have grave doubts about his love.

Does he show some public display of affection?

Even men who say they had always avoided holding hands in public or good-bye kisses on the street tell researchers that they began to do both when they fell in love. And, they said, it came easily.

> Ted was a television star. A soap opera star—*the* soap opera star. He spent twelve years smiling for the paparazzi, always with a woman at his side. He'd help them out of cars, lead them into theaters, carry their playbills, order for them at restaurants, dance with them at galas, and whisper to them at dinner parties. But he never, ever locked a lip or stroked an arm in public. He had decided long ago that his female fans were the most important women in his life, and he didn't want to give them any competition. *Once they're jealous or find me fickle, it's all over,* he worried. And then came Kim. Ted couldn't wait to show her off to the paparazzi. He held her hand, kissed her cheek, and pulled her to him for every photo. He loved her and just knew his fans would love her, too. Actually, his fans were not thrilled with Kim, nor would they be with any woman he loved, but they

> were thrilled that their hero turned out to be such a loving, giving guy after all. So Kim and Ted are married, and Ted is still *the* soap star, to this day.

What about those men who save all their loving for times behind closed doors? Are they just shy? Not ready? Too polite? Maybe. But maybe they're trying to hide their relationship with you to keep their options open.

> In Megan's case, Phil's lack of public displays of affection was the only clue that he wasn't into her. When they were alone, he couldn't stop touching her and kissing her, but when they went out in public he barely let their fingers accidentally touch when reaching for the bread basket at dinner. He wasn't even responsive when she touched him. He stiffened up when she put her hand on his back or tried to hold his hands. It took a while, but she finally got clued in that he didn't want the world to know they were together. He didn't want to make that public declaration that they were a couple. She told him she needed more, and left. He called her to tell her that he'd give her more and that he only now realized how he felt about her. "How can you love me more when I'm not with you than when I am?" she asked. "Absence makes the heart grow fonder," he said. "That's not the kind of heart I want," she said. And that was that.

Not all men will show public affection in the same way, of course. But as Megan's mother used to say, "It's not the words, it's the music that counts." And the next guy sang a very different tune. He wasn't a big hugger or a public kisser, but he loved it when she reached for his hand and held her very close when they danced. And on her birthday, he sent her a card signed "Love." When he walked into her apartment the next evening to take her to dinner with her parents, he looked for the card and said he was disappointed that it wasn't on display. Megan propped it up on the cocktail table so fast that he laughed, and she knew she had a clue to his heart.

Rx: If he's said "I love you" but is still avoiding putting the "L" word on paper, he's not fully committed.

Does he talk about the future?

If he does and you are included, take it as a clear sign that he's falling in love. There are lots of reasons why. First, people in love find that their sense of the past dims and they spend a great deal of time fantasizing about the future instead. Next, he mentions what's ahead for the two of you because the present is so great that he wants to make sure it lasts into the future. Finally, love is programmed to make us want to make a commitment and start a family.

Just think about the last time you were in love. Didn't

your childhood belief in fairy godmothers and happily-ever-afters reemerge? Wasn't every coincidence more proof of mystical "meant-to-be's"? Your guy should feel the same way if he's in love. If he doesn't, move on without him, because moving on with him will be an uphill climb!

16 How to Make Him More Perfect—for You

You've found the guy. He's lovable and he loves you. Great! But there are a few things about your Mr. Right that don't seem so, well, right. Not to worry. First of all, remember that there is no perfect man . . . in the whole world. Even your guy. Second, remember that every man you meet will be imperfect. By now you know this. But here's the very good news: Even the most imperfect man can become more perfect—for you. Not "perfect," not "more perfect"; I'm saying more perfect *for you*. And the process will feel natural and easy.

First, let me tell you what I'm not saying. I'm not saying that you can take any guy, wave a magic wand, and make him into your dream man. Sorry. I'm not saying that you can improve a guy. Only he can do that. I'm not even saying that you're going to change the things you hate about him. This isn't *Extreme Makeover: Boyfriend Edition*. You're not playing with his head. You're not training him. And you're not programming him.

What can you do, then? You can take a guy who is generally good for you and help bring out qualities he already seems to have, so he's even better for you. Why? Because that will make you even happier with the relationship. The happier you are, the happier he is and the happier you are as a twosome. If he loves you and finds you perfectly lovable, he's going to want to be more perfect for you.

I've used this approach for more than a decade to help couples. It's a powerful process, and my patients tell me that, more than any other lesson they have learned from me, this one has increased their happiness with their mate.

Here's How You Do It

1. Start by thinking about one thing you want to tweak about him

Do you want him to be a better listener when he's with you? More romantic? More talkative with you? More generous to you? More spontaneous with you? Skip the idea of changing behavior that's unrelated to you (like making him more patient with his brother) or developing behavior he has no capacity for (like making him him more interested in cooking or the kind of guy who woos a crowd with his witty personality if he doesn't have one). Pick your battles. Think to yourself: *Which one thing really matters most to me? What's a priority?*

Let's say your answer is this: "I want him to listen more when I talk. He's a great dancer, fun to be around, and makes me laugh, but he tunes out when I'm telling him about my day, my family, my friends, or my feelings. I never feel as though I've got his full attention when I'm telling a story." Maybe he's distracted. Maybe he's worried. Maybe he has an attention deficit disorder. It doesn't matter. Whatever the reason, listening isn't his strong suit. Maybe he's that way with everyone. But it matters only that he's that way with you. You've decided that he'd be more perfect for you if he was a better listener with you.

2. Next, wait for a moment when he gives you even the tiniest bit of the behavior you're looking for

Don't ask for it, but wait until it pops up spontaneously, even accidentally. For example, wait until one evening your guy gives you the kind of undivided, good listening attention that you've wanted from him. It might not be when you're telling a story, but when you're talking about a subject that he likes. It might not last very long. It might not even be on purpose, such as when you're waiting for the waiter to bring food and there's no menu to read or TV over the bar to watch. The important point is that for the moment he finally isn't distracted, interrupting you, or changing the subject. Maybe he's even asking you good follow-up questions or showing true interest in your answers, but that much isn't necessary.

3. See that little inch he's giving you? Take it a mile

How? The minute he shows you that little piece of what you want—in this case the ability to be a good listener—you let him know it. At that instant, turn to him and say, "One of the things I *love* about you is the way you listen when I talk."

What does this do? You're not only letting him know how you would like him to act toward you but showing him that he actually already has that ability. You're using it as an opportunity to label him "a good listener." You're helping him see himself as a good listener. Think of it this way: Your comments are a little mirror that reflects back the quality you'd like to see more of. He now knows that you see him as having this good quality. Soon he'll start to see himself as having it.

What you shouldn't say when you get that bit of behavior you want is just as important as what you should say. Don't say, "It's nice to see you're finally listening" or "It's about time you really listened to what I was saying" or "You've always been such a bad listener—what's changed?" Those kinds of comments are complaints disguised as compliments.

Instead, give him feedback, and the feedback is talking about what you love about him. You're not telling him he was a bad listener. You're not telling him it bugs you. Actually, you're doing the opposite. You're letting him know that you see this ability of his to listen to you. You just *love* this about him, and it means a lot. Truth is, if he listened well when you told him about the movie you saw last night, he really does have the ability to listen well to anything you say. You just need to bring that out.

I'll admit that the first time you do this and praise a behavior that he's not typically praised for, he's going to scratch his head. He's going to think, *I'm a good listener? No ex-girlfriend ever told me that. My coworkers never tell me that. In fact, they always say that's one of my worst qualities.* This is an important part of the process. It means he's really heard what you've said—something that's unique and maybe even something he's wished others had said. (Chances are, if you want to change something about him, like listening, someone else probably did, too.) This kind of feedback is registering with him—trust me.

You're also pointing out something that's very important to you, and if your guy finds you perfectly lovable, he's going to want to do things that mean a lot to you. Especially if he realizes that he is already doing these things—that you're not asking him to overhaul his personality. You haven't asked him to change a thing (which guys hate and which is unrealistic anyway). Plus, you're letting him know that you see capacities in him that are perfect for you. Not only will he feel better about himself but he'll feel better about you, too. Research on why we're attracted to some people and can't stand others is clear: We're drawn to people who make us feel marvelous about ourselves and feel an aversion toward anyone who makes us feel lousy. You're making him feel marvelous.

4. Now do it again—Wait for another moment when he shows you this thing that you really want to bring out in him

In this case, it's another instance of listening in a way that's close to or exactly what you want. Just as you did the first time, seize the moment and give him feedback. Once again, label him a good listener and let him know that you love that in him. Hold up that psychological mirror so he can see for himself that he's being a good listner. His skepticism about his being a good listener will conflict with the evidence you're showing him, and he may begin to suspect that you could be right.

5. When a third similar moment pops up, do the same as before

Notice it, label it, and give him positive feedback about how you love this ability of his and what it means to you. They say the third time is usually the charm, and in this case it's often true.

By the third time you point out to your guy that he's being a good listener, for example, he'll realize that despite what his mother, teachers, and ex-girlfriends said, he really does have the capacity to listen well and that you notice it. He'll realize that the first two times you commented on it weren't random, weren't flukes, and that you weren't delusional. He'll definitely be more aware of it and make an effort to listen more often. After three times, he'll probably start to see himself as a good listener and actually pride himself on it. He'll begin to listen actively to you because it's something that's become simple for him. You're not asking him to do a thing or to change a thing. You're just asking him to be himself.

6. Going forward, reinforce the behavior you want, but don't do it every time!

This step may surprise you. Do it just every once in a while—intermittently.

Why? Let's take our "good listener" as an example. If you commented every time he put on his listening ears—and hopefully he'd be doing it more and more—you'd run the risk of sounding silly, repetitive, and obvious, and he'd be used to providing "good listening" mainly for the praise. Then, the moment you stopped or forgot, he'd notice and stop, too.

Reacting intermittently, on the other hand, sends a different message. It lets him know that the behavior is so expected that it doesn't rate constant comment but that it's so important and appreciated that if he keeps it up, he will be rewarded for it eventually. This is how real life works. As children, we don't always get A's or presents or candy or money every single time we do well—but if we keep trying, we do get a payoff eventually. So as adults, although we don't get a raise or praise every single time we do well, we keep trying because we've learned that a reward is in our future.

If you want an example of the power of intermittent feedback, just think about gambling behavior. We don't get a win or a jackpot every time we pull the slot machine handle, but we keep throwing money into the machine because we think the payoff will come at some point. And that's why the "good listener" will keep listening—he knows eventually he'll get a payoff, too—your happy face and that psychological mirror reflecting a great image.

> Lauren loved almost everything about Mark except for his tendency to be on the cheap side. He didn't surprise her with presents or take her away on vacations. Even going out to dinner was a big deal. What bothered her wasn't really the money or lack of goodies but the feeling that he didn't want to share things with her. One night they went to the movies. He bought her ticket and handed it to her. Though it was all of seven dollars, she saw opportunity knocking. She planted a big kiss on him and said, "When you take me to the movies you make me feel like I'm a teenager on a date—like you're taking care of me, you know? Thanks." Though he looked bewildered, he seemed happy to get a compliment that clearly he'd never heard before. Shortly after that, they were out to dinner with one of his clients at a very upscale restaurant, and though it wasn't just the two of them and it was a work event, she tried the same tact. She said, "I love when you take me out to someplace luxurious like this. You make me feel very special." Then, when he picked up a plant for his mother on their way to Thanksgiving dinner, she said, "Isn't that sweet. You're so generous."

Slowly she saw his behavior change. Not only did he shed some of his stingy ways and become more generous with material things like nice dinners and gifts; he became more generous emotionally. He gave her compliments more often. Instead of always rushing her, he seemed to have more patience. The funny part? He started boasting to other people about his generous ways. He loved this new side of himself and ran with it.

The important thing to remember is that this wasn't about changing Mark's personality or making him a better person. It wasn't about playing with his head or trying to make him over, either. It was about bringing out a quality that he already had some capacity for. Lauren saw a tiny glimpse of it, showed it to him with her feedback, and let him know how important it was to her. She made him see that he had the ability to do something she loved. She also made him see that he could make her even happier without having to change a thing.

More Ways to Make Him More Perfect for You

As I've said before, you don't have to have the same interests in order to connect with someone. In fact, different interests can actually be healthy. But research finds that quantity of time together is as important as quality of time together for couples. So why not introduce your guy to some of the things you love and see if he likes them, too? For example, you love to ski, so one weekend you take him on a ski trip. He's never hit the slopes before, but he's willing to give it a try. After just a few runs on the bunny hill, hopefully he's hooked. He's got an interest in one of your interests, and now it can be something you do together. Now he's even more involved in your life, and that connection may strengthen what you have. It may not always work out like this. You may take him to a poetry reading and he'll fall asleep. Or you'll take him to the gym and he'll hate it. It doesn't mean your relationship is any worse off, but it was worth a try to see if things would work out the other way.

Of course, you can try to pick up some of his interests, too. Sharing his hobbies can also make him more perfect for you. But this is not a recommendation to force any pastime down your own throat or "change" for him. It's just a suggestion that you might find something for you through him. Then you've increased your time together and widened your own horizon.

And you can also make him more perfect for you by reviewing from time to time all the guys who came before him. If they missed by a mile, his misses may seem unimportant by comparison. Like Grandma said, the glass is half full or half empty—it's up to you. Cognitive psychologists now say the same thing, and their studies find that you can turn around a depression or a relationship by turning around your perspective. Remember . . .

Rx: What you think is not the result of how you feel; it's the cause of how you feel.

How much change, however, can anyone really expect? Only those changes that we have the capacity and motivation to make. Take yourself as an example. You can choose to change how you behave, of course, if you decide to be more forceful or frivolous or affectionate. You can choose to change how you think, too, if the primary principle leads you to change how you see yourself and others. You can even choose to change what you say to men, to your friends, and to your family if it's in your best interest, as long as you are treating them with the respect and consideration you would want, too. But you can't change who you are, so don't even try.

You are a mix of your temperament, your knowledge, your experiences, your talents, your challenges, your vulnerabilities, your feedback, your traumas, and your victories. As with a cake, the ingredients can't be changed once they're all baked together. Add a layer if you want. Ice it. Decorate it. But most of all, enjoy it!

And as for his cake—it's also already baked. Too late to add more sugar or salt to the batter. If it's not your taste, don't try to remix it. You'll end up with crumbs. Acquire a taste, or save your appetite for the next one.

17 Love His Flaws

So far, we've talked about when to give it a try with a guy and when to run screaming for the exit. We've talked about meeting him halfway and how to tell just how imperfect he is. By now you probably feel pretty comfortable with the primary principle "It's not you, it's him," as well as the basic assumptions. Hopefully they've become your mantra:

Assume that you're perfect as you are . . . perfectly lovable, that is!

Assume that you're entitled, therefore, to be loved by a perfect man.

Assume, however, that there is no perfect man in the whole world, and every man you meet will be "imperfect"—in many ways.

So now I'm going to add another basic assumption to the mix:

Assume that once you've decided that he's perfectly lovable anyway—no complaining!

His quirks may drive you crazy, but you've decided that they aren't bad enough to drive you away. That's the key—making that decision. Take as long as you need to be sure that you want him despite his quirks. There are definitely characteristics that make him less than perfect. But once you've decided that he's still for you, you're in a no-complaining zone—for your sake, for his sake, and for the sake of everyone around you.

Quirks are not the warning signs we discussed in Chapter 10, like abuse, jealousy that is out of bounds, lying, cheating, and so on. Those are the kinds of problems you should never put up with in a relationship—zero tolerance! Zero!

Quirks are also not the issues we discussed in Chapter 11, like unfinished business and relationship amnesia. Those are issues that couples therapists warn are cause for concern, and they should at least make you really consider whether you should move forward with this person.

But even if the guy you're dating doesn't show any of those serious behavioral problems or traits, he'll still have quirks. He is a man, after all, and thus presumptively imperfect. So though there are many things that you may love about him, starting with his finding *you* perfectly lovable, there are other things that can irritate you no end.

Men and Their Quirks

By quirks, we're talking about habits like leaving the toilet seat up or wet towels on the bedroom floor. We're talking about attitudes like the sexist jokes he tells and things you complain to your girlfriends about when you're having lunch or girls' night out. We're talking about personality traits that you just can't change, such as when he anticipates the worst instead of the best. And we're talking about those *universal* male peculiarities, too, such as his refusing to ask for directions or let you drive the car when you travel together, even when it's your car.

If your "plus vs. minus" list or your gut feelings tell you that he's a keeper anyway, it's time to accept the faults as part of the package. Constantly reacting to them as if they are new creates unnecessary stress for you and tension for him. Tom Cruise is short—just part of the package. So don't fret every time you pass up a pair of high heels to go on a date with him.

Diane understands this. She worked for years in public relations and says she's learned how to put a positive spin on anything.

> When Diane became seriously involved with Carl, she realized early on that he was not a planner or a

> details kind of guy. His head was often at work, and she ended up picking the restaurants, calling their friends, making the plans. She told herself, *This is my chance to turn back. But if I don't and I accept him the way he is, then there's no going back. I will never complain about this again.* Carl and Diane eventually married and Carl's inattention to details still bugs Diane at times. But she chooses to turn what could be negative thoughts about Carl into positive ones—Carl's focus on his job has made him a leader in his field and given them a comfortable lifestyle that lets her be a stay-at-home mom to their three children.

Diane could not change Carl's behavior, but she could change her own perspective on it. She made it a positive. She made herself happy. That made Carl happy, too.

Take the Package Deal

Ask any woman involved in a long-term relationship if her guy has habits that drive her nuts and she'll probably say, "How much time have you got?" We all have our quirks (even perfectly lovable women), but we've decided to accept his as part of the package. So how do you stop complaining? How do you live with those shortcomings day to day without wanting to scream? The answer is this:

Rx: You don't have to like his quirks—just don't take them personally!

Actually, this is the secret to all interpersonal survival. If you can't change someone's action, change your reaction. Remind yourself that he's not purposely doing it to irritate you—really, he's not. Observe him as if you were not involved at all, but as if you were a behavioral scientist studying a case. Or a movie writer studying a character. You may find that he does the things he does because he's preoccupied, even oblivious, or because it's important enough to him to continue doing. You don't have to like the quirk—just don't take it personally.

Caroline doesn't take it personally.

> Caroline's boyfriend hates to shave. Absolutely hates it. He doesn't have the kind of job for which he must shave every day, so when he whips out the shaving cream and razors, Caroline knows he's got a business meeting to attend. If there's no meeting for a while, the whiskers grow until he can't stand them. Early on in the relationship, Caroline mentioned that she liked him clean-shaven. She tried to appeal to his vanity, telling him he looked handsomer, younger, and slimmer when he shaved (all true). But he said it was his face and he hated to shave often. Caroline decided that she could

> constantly be mad about this and pick fights over it, or she could just accept it as one of his quirks and live with it. Since Caroline and her boyfriend are otherwise very compatible, she keeps quiet about the shaving.

Sometimes his quirks are just products of the way he was raised, and seeing his quirks that way can help. Does Jessie's story sound familiar to you?

> Whenever Jessie and Bob are going somewhere, Bob is ready before Jessie—way before Jessie. So even though they are not running late, he starts making her rush around and goes out to start the car before Jessie has finished getting herself ready. Then he's mad at her for not being ready "on time." They're both in a grumpy mood during the ride, and Jessie has inevitably forgotten something in the mad dash to get out to the car. "I can't live this way," Jessie complained to everyone who'd listen. She felt pressured and defensive until she and Bob's family went to an anniversary party together. She watched Bob's father do the same thing to his whole family, and heard Bob's mother say "Yes, dear" a few times—but then not rush! Now she sees the early-bird act as a family trait and tries to just go with the flow.

Sometimes you can actually turn down the volume of your annoyance by behaving as you would if the quirk didn't bother you—not for his sake, but for yours. Here's how it works. If you ignore your annoyance, skip the pleas for sympathy from your friends, and spare the guy your critical reaction, the quirk will become less important in your life. You won't be reviewing it, talking about it, and gathering similar stories. When you don't make use of your annoyance or the adrenaline that fuels it, you'll produce less and less of it.

Rx: Make peace with traits you can't change in others or you'll be at war with them forever.

Pause for Perspective

If you're still not sure if you can really stop complaining, but want to, try to think your way out of annoyance by imagining love lost. It's very powerful and effective, but like any strong medicine, save it for when you really need it.

You know how we all say when we're going for a serious medical test, "If I'm okay, I'll never sweat the small stuff again"? Well, think of his flaws as the "small stuff." Or imagine that *he's* going for the serious medical tests. That should help put his quirks into perspective.

I'm not recommending that we go around constantly fantasizing about cataclysmic events to shake us up and realign our perspective on "small stuff," but I am recommending that you do it from time to time to regain the big picture. Enjoy the view!

18 Love the New You

The new you looks just like the old you, laughs like the old you, and sighs like the old you. The new you didn't have to change a hair or a hem. The new you is different in only one way. The new you has changed your view. What does that mean?

It means that you see being single as a fact, not a fault.

It means that you have traded the myth of male perfection for the math of probabilities.

It means that you show zero tolerance for guys who give you zero.

It means that you no longer try to change yourself for anyone but you.

It means that you try to please yourself more, to encourage the men you meet to please you, too.

It means that you remember that *everything a guy may say or do is information about him, not you!*

The new you won't settle for less than guys who find you perfectly lovable *as you are!*

The new you falls wildly in love with one of those guys and makes him feel lovable, too, quirks and all.

And most of all, the new you knows that if he doesn't think you're perfectly lovable, it's his loss, not yours. You no longer even ask why. You just say to yourself: "It's not me, it's him!"

about the author

GEORGIA WITKIN, PH.D., one of the nation's foremost authorities on women and stress, is the director of The Stress Program at the Mount Sinai Medical Center in New York City, where she is an assistant clinical professor of psychiatry and assistant professor of obstetrics, gynecology, and reproductive sciences. On the Fox News Channel, she is the lifestyle contributor to *Fox Magazine* and a news analyst on the *Fox and Friends* morning program. She has also appeared as the nightly health reporter on WNBC, show host on CNBC, and a guest expert on *The Oprah Winfrey Show*, *20/20*, CBS News, CNN, Court TV, the *Today* show, *Live with Regis and Kelly*, and more than one hundred other programs. Her articles and quotes have appeared in a multitude of publications, including *Time*, *Newsweek*, *USA Today*, and the *New York Times*. In addition, Witkin has written nine books, among them *The Female Stress Survival Guide*, *The Male Stress Survival Guide*, *Kidstress*, *The Truth About Women*, and *Stress Relief for Disasters Great and Small*. She has served on the boards of the *Journal of Preventative Psychiatry*, *Mental Health*, *Woman Magazine*, *Brides* magazine, and *Health* magazine. She lives in New York City.